"Be ye holy"

The Call to Christian Separation

fred moritz

 **Bob Jones University Press**
Greenville, South Carolina 29614

Library of Congress Cataloging-in-Publication Data

Moritz, Fred, 1942-
   "Be ye holy": the call to Christian separation / Fred Moritz.
     p. cm.
   Includes bibliographical references and index.
   ISBN 0-89084-737-1
   1. Separation from sin—Christianity.   2. Fundamentalism.
   I. Title.
   BT82.2.M67   1994
   234'.8—dc20   93-50169
                                                       CIP

NOTE:
The fact that materials produced by other publishers are referred to in this volume does not constitute an endorsement by Bob Jones University Press of the content or theological position of materials produced by such publishers. The position of Bob Jones University Press, and the University itself, is well known. Any references and ancillary materials are listed as an aid to the reader and in an attempt to maintain the accepted academic standards of the publishing industry.

"Be Ye Holy": The Call to Christian Separation
by Fred Moritz

Cover designed by Brian Johnson
Edited by Mark Sidwell

© 1994 Bob Jones University Press
Greenville, South Carolina 29614

Printed in the United States of America

ISBN 0-89084-737-1

15   14   13   12   11   10 9 8 7 6 5 4 3 2 1

CONTENTS

FOREWORD

Dr. Fred Moritz has done a great favor for those of us who hold the Bible to be the infallible Word of God and believe that God requires a separated and holy life of those who are saved by His grace. It is also a favor for those who may be confused about this matter.

He has brought together the many passages of Scripture that declare this fact and has shown that there is no conflict between salvation by grace alone and the requirement of a holy life.

Dr. Moritz uses the opinions of godly and brilliant scholars and saints throughout history to show that God requires not only personal holiness but also ecclesiastical separation.

This is one of only a few books on ecclesiastical separation written by true evangelicals. The pens of neo-evangelicals have been very prolific on the subject from an opposing viewpoint.

It is good to have a logical, scholarly, biblical treatise on this subject from the pen of a strong evangelist, leader, and servant of missionaries.

May God bless this book as it goes forth from the press!

Monroe Parker, Ph.D., D.D., LL.D.
General Director
Baptist World Mission

PREFACE

My spiritual roots grow deep in the rich soil of a godly heritage. German immigrant grandparents knew Christ as their Savior and reared nine children. As far as I know, all nine of those children came to Christ and are in heaven. I am told that my grandfather, who died before my birth, stood over my dad's cradle and prayed that God would call him to preach. Dad became a structural iron worker, but he had an encyclopedic knowledge of the Scriptures. I have concluded that my grandfather's prayers were answered in the next generation. My mother's parents also knew the Lord, and Granddad possessed a hatred for sin that was as fierce as it was holy. His life reflected an intimate daily walk with the Lord. My mother is a living saint. Her sweet influence affects her children, grand-children, and a great number of her former Primary Department Sunday school kids. Several of them are in the Lord's work today.

One of the influences of my heritage is separatism. My dad developed some strong convictions about personal and ecclesiastical separation. He was saved at the age of twenty-five, but some of his "worldly" habits hung on for a time. Shortly after I was born, he stayed home from church with me so that Mother could attend Sunday services on a day when the weather was inclement. Toward the end of that week it dawned upon my mother that the ashtrays were removed from the house. He had apparently decided on that Lord's Day that he did not want me to be influenced by his smoking and stopped smoking on the spot. When television became popular, he never bought one. He was fearful that we would be unduly influenced by the violence in the programming, and that was in the 1950s! I wonder what he would think now. It is amazing that my sister and I never felt deprived, and we never reacted against our "strict fundamentalist" upbringing. Perhaps we did not reject what we learned in the home because we saw our parents demonstrate a consistent and genuine Christian lifestyle.

For some years my parents attended the German Baptist church (part of the North American Baptist General Conference) in which Dad had grown up. Two men in the church, one the janitor and one the chairman of the deacons, shared a common practice—each man smoked a cigar. On Sunday morning they would place their partially smoked cigars on opposite ends of the same brick ledge as they entered the building. One Lord's Day, Dad waited until the men had parked their "stogies" and entered the building, and then he switched the cigars!

Modernism was taking over the churches, and the pastor began to say that the new birth is "turning over a new leaf" rather than the regenerating work of the Holy Spirit. My parents left the church and eventually joined a small, growing, Bible-preaching Baptist church. We attended that church for years; I have fond memories of it.

God led me to Pillsbury Baptist Bible College when high school was completed. God's grace was abundant there. I trusted Christ and also came under the influence of Pillsbury's president, Dr. Monroe Parker. I esteem him as a scholar, preacher, teacher, counselor, close friend, and, since 1981, both mentor and boss. We have been friends since 1958.

Part of Dr. Parker's multifaceted influence has been his sane, kind, militant, unwavering commitment to biblical separatism. The issue of Billy Graham's ecumenical evangelism was prominent while I was in college. During those four years I also witnessed the intense debate over New Evangelicalism in the Conservative Baptist movement, with which my home church and Pillsbury were both identified. I saw Dr. Parker help lead the battle against the compromise of biblical principles in those struggles. He taught, preached, and practiced *biblical separation as a complement of biblical evangelism*. He also walked with God, lived a consistent lifestyle, led many people to Christ, and encouraged local churches and pastors. He exemplified what the Bible says a Christian and a preacher should be.

God next placed me at Central Baptist Seminary in Minneapolis under the influence of Dr. Richard V. Clearwaters. He was a genuine intellectual, a tenderhearted pastor, a fervent soulwinner, and a militant separatist. He and the professors there demonstrated thorough scholarship, a warm evangelistic spirit, and consistent separatism.

In more recent years I have had the privilege of studying at Bob Jones University. There I have been challenged by men who have some of the finest minds I know. They also exhibit a love for the souls of men, a gracious Christian spirit, and an unwavering commitment to the truth revealed in the Scriptures. This book is the result of my research and writing project at the University.

Reviewing my heritage is not mere reflection. I grew up in a heritage in which my family loved the Lord, honored His Word, and practiced separation. My training for the ministry convinced me that there is a biblical basis for the practice of separation. My further study of the Scriptures over these years in the gospel ministry has confirmed that conviction in my mind. I believe that the Bible teaches separation and that its teachings are clear, unequivocal, and discernible. There is a "theology of separation" set forth in Holy Scripture.

I pray that God will use this study of the Scriptures to persuade others as I have been persuaded. I pray that those who are persuaded as I am will be encouraged to continue to be faithful to the Lord. I pray that we will see that separation is not sufficient of itself but must be linked to evangelism. I pray that we will see that separation demands both a biblical practice and a biblical spirit.

INTRODUCTION

Biblical separation has been an issue of intense debate and contention in American Christianity since 1947. After the modernist-fundamentalist controversy of the first half of the twentieth century, a new movement arose in the middle of the century. That movement was identified by its advocates as New Evangelicalism.

Harold John Ockenga succinctly stated the difference between fundamentalism and New Evangelicalism. "Dr. Ockenga pointed out . . . that the strategy of the New Evangelicalism has changed from one of separation to infiltration."[1] That statement described one of the distinctives of the New Evangelical movement. Twenty-one years later, in introducing Lindsell's book *The Battle for the Bible,* Ockenga recalled his 1948 address at the opening of Fuller Theological Seminary. He reiterated, "While reaffirming the theological view of fundamentalism, this address repudiated its ecclesiology and its social theory. The ringing call for a repudiation of separatism and the summons to social involvement received a hearty response from many evangelicals."[2] Neff states, "The fledgling movement eschewed the intellectual obscurantism and ecclesiastical separatism characteristic of much fundamentalism."[3] The adherents to the New Evangelical philosophy have known and embraced this repudiation of separatism to this day.

In 1957 New Evangelicalism caught the public eye with Evangelist Billy Graham's public embrace of cooperative evangelism and the issuing of Ockenga's press release outlining the New Evangelical philosophy. Since that time, the New Evangelicals have clearly stated their repudiation of separatism. That repudiation has,

1

in fact, been a major distinctive of the movement. Fundamentalists have consistently affirmed separatism as a biblical principle. They assert that separatism cannot be repudiated as a strategy because it is founded in biblical theology and is plainly commanded by Scripture.

The New Evangelicals are now concerned that their movement "may be less certain of its direction and identity."[4] It appears also that some younger fundamentalists have lost some of the vision, discernment, and direction that characterized their forerunners who refused to follow Ockenga's call to repudiate separatism. Having lost the historical perspective on the struggle and lacking an understanding of the biblical principles which produce the practice of separatism, many appear to be adrift. They lack a frame of reference for practicing separatism.

This book deals with the subject of separation—its biblical foundations and guidelines for its practice. The first chapter will examine the Old Testament and New Testament words for holiness. It will seek to show that the concept of separation from sin is part of the idea of holiness and will outline the Bible's teaching concerning the holiness of God. Our thesis is that the holiness of God is the foundation of all separation, whether personal or ecclesiastical. Therefore, the overall purpose of this chapter will be to provide a biblical frame of reference for the philosophy and practice of separatism.

Succeeding chapters will deal with personal separation, ecclesiastical separation, separation from errant or disobedient Christian brothers, and the spirit of the separatist.

Since the focus of this book is on biblical principles and guidelines, it will not seek merely to "name names." Our purpose is not to identify current New Evangelicals or to discuss transitory issues but to identify permanent biblical principles by which one may evaluate issues and men's actions. It will be necessary to identify men who advocate certain positions, but such identification will be incidental to the focus on principles and guidelines. We seek to create a frame of reference for thought and action.

This book seeks to achieve several specific goals. First, it seeks to refocus fundamentalists. No human movement is perfect. Perhaps succeeding generations of separatists have become disillusioned because fundamentalism seems to have focused on personalities more than principle. Some may react against a perceived harshness of spirit in some separatist leaders. Others may weary of the need for perpetual vigilance and militancy, or be discouraged with spokesmen whose focus "goes to seed." When a ministry's emphasis shifts from separatism as the complement of evangelism to separatism as an end in itself, that ministry is deadened. Separatists must fear and avoid all of these dangers. However, if separatism is based on God's holiness and is commanded in Scripture, then it is the right position. The response of succeeding generations of separatists should be to seek a biblical balance in their ministries and to commit themselves anew to the biblical strategy.

Second, this book intends to challenge those who have grown up in the New Evangelical frame of reference. We will reiterate in these pages that Ockenga and those after him articulated the rejection of separatism as one of their distinctives. They will say that the basic division between fundamentalists and New Evangelicals took place over the issue of separatism.

New Evangelicals repudiate separation; fundamentalists embrace it. Both premises cannot be correct. Someone has erred in this debate. If separatism is a biblically grounded strategy, then New Evangelicalism rests on a false premise. It follows that dialogue and cooperation with theological apostates for over four decades have greatly weakened the cause of Christ. If separation is not a biblical strategy, then separatists have wrought harmful and unnecessary divisions among believers.

This book challenges the reader to take a hard look at the distinctives of New Evangelicalism and to examine the roots of the movement. Those who will honestly evaluate the biblical evidence will find themselves driven to conclude that the separatist strategy of the fundamentalists is valid.

This challenge is appropriate at this time. Neff cites several reasons for the lack of clear direction within New Evangelicalism:

> Those inside challenges? First, the moral lapses of both administrators of parachurch organizations and stars of evangelical show biz; second, the inevitable fuzziness that develops around the edges of truth commitments when a movement puts energy and effort into higher education, with its fussy passion for qualification and careful nuance; and third, the "Half-Way Covenant" factor that obtains

> when a new generation comes to leadership that has called
> neo-evangelicalism its family but does not itself bear the scars
> of the original battles fought to preserve the truth.[5]

I must hasten to make two observations. First, the New Evangelicals possess no monopoly on moral failures. *All* moral failures are directly related to the subject of biblical separation. This book will deal with a subject that no other book on separation has dealt with to my knowledge—the subject of personal separation. We will demonstrate that personal separation and ecclesiastical separation *cannot* be divorced because both take root in the holiness of God. Second, we must observe that the battles the New Evangelicals fought with the fundamentalists were not to preserve but to repudiate what we understand to be scriptural truth: namely, the biblical teaching on separation.

Third, this book intends to call for change. Some biblical separatists need to reorient their focus. Separation is not an end in itself. Scripture declares that separation complements evangelism; separation that is not wedded to fervent evangelism produces a sterile orthodoxy. That kind of separatism needs to be forsaken! Separatists need to examine the criteria by which they separate from other believers and must make sure that biblical principles, not personality conflicts, guide such actions. Separatists must evaluate their attitudes by the standard of the revealed Word.

This book calls for fundamental and radical change on the part of those who repudiate separatism. Separation derives from God's holiness. When believers must separate from other believers, issues of holiness are the reasons for such separation. The spirit of the separatist is largely molded by the idea of holiness. If these claims are demonstrably true, then New Evangelicalism's basic premise is fatally flawed. Its adherents must make an objective, biblical appraisal. There is no biblical alternative but to forsake an unbiblical strategy of cooperation with unbelievers and return to a biblical practice of separation.

I confess that I cannot bring about the changes for which I call. Paul revealed the source of spiritual change with these words: "But we all, with open face beholding as in a glass the glory of the Lord, are changed into the same image from glory to glory, even as by the Spirit of the Lord" (II Cor. 3:18).

I ask you to examine the biblical evidence with an open mind and heart. I pray that the Spirit of God will teach the truth of the Word of God and work the needed changes in each life and ministry.

Notes

[1] Harold John Ockenga, Press Release, 8 December 1957, Boston, The Park Street Church, p. 2. See Appendix B, pp. 117-19, for the full text of the press release.

[2] Harold John Ockenga, Introduction to *The Battle for the Bible,* by Harold Lindsell. (Grand Rapids: Zondervan, 1976), p. 11.

[3] David Neff, "A Good First Step," *Christianity Today*, 14 July 1989, p. 15.

[4] Ibid.

[5] Ibid.

1

HOLINESS—
THE FOUNDATION OF SEPARATION

One of the most critical parts of any building project is the construction of the foundation. It must be square and solid and placed upon soil that can sustain it. When I was in my first pastorate, we built a new auditorium. The contractor came to dig the basement and pour the footings. He followed the blueprints exactly as they had been drawn as he staked out the building, dug the hole, and began to place the forms for the footers. As he proceeded, he sensed that something was not right. The building appeared to be narrower at one end than at the other. He checked the blueprints and discovered that the engineer who drew them had made a mistake: his design had the building one foot too narrow on one end. He made the correction and the construction job went on successfully. Had he not noticed that mistake, we would have had a lot of grief to correct it after the concrete had been poured. We might have ended up with a funny looking Baptist church building! My dad spent his life as a structural iron worker. He used to say that architects *never* make mistakes, they just make changes!

This chapter is as important to this book as the foundation is to a building. The practice of separation must rest on a solid biblical foundation. The thesis of this book is that the holiness of God is the foundation of all separation, whether personal or ecclesiastical.

Scripture demonstrates a natural relationship between holiness and separation. That means that when men imitate God's holiness they forsake, or separate from, thoughts and actions which are sinful and contrary to God's holiness. A survey of the biblical teaching on holiness shows that holiness demands separation from unbelief and sin. One could say separation flows from, or is the natural result of, the Bible's teaching on holiness. This relationship between holiness and separation will be demonstrated in succeeding chapters.

We must understand another more basic fact when we deal with separation. Separation not only results in holiness but also is an *integral part* of holiness. Separation is the natural outgrowth of holiness because it is a part of the essential concept of holiness. One cannot stress the idea of holiness as it is taught in the Bible without stressing the concept of separation as well. The philosophy and practice of separation have a biblical, theological basis.

The purpose of this chapter is to demonstrate that the idea of separation is part of the very fabric of the doctrine of holiness.

Words for Holiness

Old Testament Words

In the Old Testament the Hebrew word קֹדֶשׁ (*qodesh*) and the words related to it are used for holiness.[1] The words are translated as "pure, clean, holy."[2] The concepts of purity and separation are universally recognized by lexicographers as the essential meaning of these words. They define the words as "holy, sanctuary, cleanse, apartness, sacredness,"[3] or "be holy, withheld from profane use . . . holy things, filled with holiness, therefore to be treated carefully."[4]

Hebrew scholars generally say that these words derive from root words which mean "to cut or separate."[5] There is widespread, but not universal, agreement among them on this point. It is also possible that the words come from a root which means "shining."[6] If the latter is the case, the ideas of "purity, newness," and "freshness" are part of the definition of these words.[7] Most likely the root "to cut" is the source of the words for holiness, but the issue cannot be resolved beyond doubt. It is clear that the idea of separation is part of the Old Testament words for holiness, regardless of their original root meaning.[8]

New Testament Words

The Greek verb ἁγιάζω (*hagiazō*; "sanctify") with its cognates is "the Greek representative of Kadash."[9] A related word, ἁγνός (*hagnos*), shares the same root.[10] The fundamental idea of the word seems to be separation.[11] Two other words are used in the New Testament to convey the idea of holiness. Ὅσιος (*hosios*) conveys the idea of piety, while ἱερός (*hieros*) connotes consecration.[12]

The idea of separation is one of the aspects of the words for holiness. The Hebrew words in the Old Testament and the Greek words in the New Testament all involve separation as a part of their meanings. We will see shortly that separation is not all there is to holiness, but it is a vital part of the concept.

It is clear that the idea of separation is inherent in holiness. If a person or thing is positively pure and clean, that person or thing is also negatively set apart or separated from what is impure and unclean. With this fact established, it is necessary to see the important role of holiness in the Bible's teaching concerning the character of God.

The Holiness of God

Charles C. Ryrie defines God's holiness when he says, "In respect to God, holiness means not only that He is separate from all that is unclean and evil, but also that He is positively pure and thus distinct from all others."[13] A. H. Strong calls God's holiness His "self-affirming purity,"[14] while G. C. Knapp states that it "is his moral perfection."[15]

Students of Scripture and theology have used several terms and descriptions to describe the holiness of God. Thomas Watson advanced four propositions on the holiness of God. He stated, "God is holy intrinsically. He is holy in His nature. His very being is made up of holiness, as light is the essence of the sun. . . . God is holy primarily. He is the original and pattern of holiness. . . . God is holy efficiently. He is the cause of all that is holy in others. . . . God is holy transcendently. No angel in heaven can take the just dimensions of God's holiness."[16]

Isaiah 57:15 stands out as a helpful verse for an analysis of God's holiness. It states, "For thus saith the high and lofty One that inhabiteth eternity, whose name is Holy; I dwell in the high and holy place, with him also that is of a contrite and humble spirit, to revive the spirit of the humble, and to revive the heart of the contrite ones." This verse outlines three basic aspects of God's holiness. It describes His (1) intrinsic holiness ("whose name is Holy"); (2) transcendent holiness ("I dwell in the high and lofty place"); and

(3) immanent holiness ("I dwell . . . with him also that is of a contrite and humble spirit").

Intrinsic Holiness

William Shedd offers a clear explanation of the idea of intrinsic holiness: "Holiness in God, must, consequently, be defined as conformity to His own perfect nature. The only rule for the divine will is the divine reason; and the divine reason prescribes everything that it is befitting an Infinite being to do. God is not under law, nor above law. He is law."[17] Holiness is essential to God's character. This is seen from several statements in Scripture.

Holy Name

The Bible repeatedly declares that God's name is holy. Statements such as "whose name is Holy" (Isa. 57:15), and "For he that is mighty hath done to me great things; and holy is his name" (Luke 1:49) are representative of many passages which declare that God's name is holy.

"Holy One"

One of the names by which God is known is the name "Holy One." This name is used of God is several places (Job 6:10; Pss. 22:3; 71:22). In a special sense He is the "Holy One of Israel" (Isa. 1:4). This title apparently refers to the holiness which resides in His very character.

Separate from Evil

That holiness is inherent in God's character is further seen by the fact that Scripture declares Him to be free of all sin and evil. Habakkuk forcefully states this fact: "Art thou not from everlasting, O Lord my God, mine Holy One? we shall not die. O Lord, thou hast ordained them for judgment; and, O mighty God, thou hast established them for correction. Thou art of purer eyes than to behold evil, and canst not look on iniquity: wherefore lookest thou upon them that deal treacherously, and holdest thy tongue when the wicked devoureth the man that is more righteous than he?" (Hab. 1:12-13). While discoursing with God about the coming judgment of Judah, Habakkuk makes "a statement of faith in the Lord's covenanted justice."[18] He grounds his hope in the holiness of God.

His trust is that God will not permit the nation to die but that the Chaldeans will be used only to execute His judgment. Because God is holy, He cannot tolerate evil. His holiness constitutes a purity which cannot countenance evil and treachery (v. 13). This fact plainly indicates that God is intrinsically holy.

Jeremiah was overwhelmed by the Lord "because of the words of his holiness" (Jer. 23:9). In direct contrast to God's holiness, he saw the land characterized by adultery and swearing. Jeremiah said of sinful men that "their course is evil, and their force is not right" (Jer. 23:10). Unlike sinful man God is holy, free from evil. Jeremiah saw man in contrast to God as *profane* (Jer. 23:11). Malachi also states that by sin "Judah hath profaned the holiness of the Lord" (Mal. 2:11). The word "profane" connotes the idea of "defiled, polluted."[19] God, by contrast, is free of all evil. Separation is revealed as a fundamental concept of holiness at this point.

Swearing in Holiness

The intrinsic holiness of God's character may be seen in the oaths He makes. Twice God states that He has sworn in His holiness (Ps. 89:35; Amos 4:2). Once He states that He has sworn in His truth (Ps. 132:11). At least four times Scripture teaches that God has sworn by Himself (Isa. 45:23; Jer. 49:13; 51:14; Amos 6:8). John Randolph Jaeggli, comparing Amos 4:2 with 6:8, draws a conclusion which is reinforced by the other Scriptures cited. He says, "The parallel structure of these two phrases draws the interpreter's attention to the equation of God's holiness with the essence of His personality."[20]

Perfect in Work

God's holiness of character is further seen by the fact that His works are perfect. Scripture teaches that "the Lord is righteous in all his ways, and holy in all his works" (Ps. 145:17). His power is declared to be holy (Ps. 98:1). His judgment is holy (Isa. 5:16), and His holiness is revealed in salvation (Isa. 52:10). Although he does not use the word *holiness,* Moses seems to summarize the fact that God's work is holy when he says "his work is perfect" (Deut. 32:4). The New Testament quotation of that statement associates holiness with God's work (Rev. 16:5).

Perfect in Virtue

Scripture not only describes God's work as holy, but also describes His virtues as being holy. The Bible declares His righteousness (Isa. 5:16) and His truthfulness to be holy (Rev. 6:10).

The Standard of Holiness in Man

From the fact that God is intrinsically holy another truth logically follows. If holiness is a part of God's character, then He alone is the standard of revealed holiness. His holiness sets the standard of conduct for men. In other words, actions are holy or unholy as they are consistent with or in violation of God's nature. Strong forcefully states, "God is holy in that He is the source and standard of the right."[21]

This fact is revealed in Leviticus 19-20. The passage begins with the demand for holiness in Israel and the affirmation that God is holy (Lev. 19:2). Then follows a long list of required actions and prohibited actions. Fifteen times in Leviticus 19 this list is reinforced with the statement "I am the Lord." God affirms His own holiness, and the reason given for a commanded or forbidden action is simply "I am the Lord." One must conclude that the action commanded reflects God's holiness and forbidden action is contrary to His holiness. This quality is both positive and negative. "Sanctify yourselves therefore, and be ye holy: for I am the Lord your God. And ye shall keep my statutes, and do them: I am the Lord which sanctify you" (Lev. 20:7-8).

The reason witchcraft is wrong is because it is contrary to God's holiness (Lev. 20:6). The reason that God's statutes are to be obeyed is because they reflect His holiness, and He set Israel apart to be holy unto Him. The same truth is reiterated in verses 24 and 26.

The holiness of God was not only the standard for human conduct for Israel, but it is also the standard for Christians. This timeless principle is repeated in the New Testament. It transcends dispensations. God's character is unchanging. "But as he which hath called you is holy, so be ye holy in all manner of conversation: Because it is written, Be ye holy; for I am holy" (I Pet. 1:15-16).

In short, God is holy in His character, and His holiness becomes the standard which determines right and wrong in human conduct. This is what Watson calls "primary holiness."[22]

Transcendent Holiness

This term conveys the understanding that God is unique in His holiness and is separate and distinct from His creation. He is exalted in holiness. When Moses and the children of Israel sang after their deliverance at the Red Sea, they praised God's transcendent holiness. They asked, "Who is like unto thee, O Lord, among the gods? Who is like thee, glorious in holiness, fearful in praises, doing wonders?" (Exod. 15:11). Hannah gladly recognized the transcendent holiness of God in her prayer: "There is none holy as the Lord: for there is none beside thee: neither is there any rock like our God" (I Sam. 2:2). The same truth is stated later in the same book: "Who is able to stand before this holy Lord God?" (I Sam. 6:20). The song of Moses and the Lamb likewise reiterates the truth: "Who shall not fear thee O Lord, and glorify thy name? for thou only art holy: for all nations shall come and worship before thee; for thy judgments are made manifest" (Rev. 15:4).

Holiness and God's Glory

God's holiness and glory are linked together several places in Scripture.[23] God is glorious in His holiness (Exod. 15:11). Because He is the Holy One, His glory covers heaven and earth (Hab. 3:3). Part of His honor, weight, substance, or worth is His holiness. For this reason He is to be praised (Hab. 3:3; I Chron. 16:29; Ps. 96:7-8). His dwelling place in heaven is said to be "the habitation of thy holiness and of thy glory" (Isa. 63:15). The tabernacle was sanctified (made holy or set apart) by the presence of God's glory in it (Exod. 29:43).

The Beauty of Holiness

Five times in the Old Testament (I Chron. 16:29; II Chron. 20:21; Pss. 29:2; 96:9; 110:3) beauty and holiness are linked. All five passages refer to the worship of God by man, and these passages also link God's glory to His holiness. Girdlestone explains the meaning of this phrase "the beauty of holiness": "Other suggested readings are 'the glorious sanctuary' and 'holy array.' The word 'beauty' frequently means majesty or excellency, and probably points to the glory of God rather than to the garments of man."[24]

The Separation Between God and Man

Clearly God is separate from His creation. He is holy in His character. No god is like Him, and He is greater than man. This division exists partly because God is the Creator and as such is greater than His creation. The condition is not just that God is intrinsically and transcendentally holy and that man is neutral. The transcendence of God is made more glaring by man's sin nature. Given the fact of God's holiness, Chestnut is accurate when he states, "To sin is to violate any of God's requirements in any way."[25] He further points out the threefold nature of sin. Sin is sin because (1) "It is self-assertion against God's will" (Gen. 3:4, 7), (2) "it breaks the bond between man and God," and (3) "because the violator loses holiness derived from closeness to God."[26] When sinful man comprehends, even in part, the holiness of God, only one response is possible. Isaiah said it for all men when he recounted: "Then said I, Woe is me! for I am undone; because I am a man of unclean lips, and I dwell in the midst of a people of unclean lips: for mine eyes have seen the King, the Lord of hosts" (Isa. 6:5).

Scripture declares that God in His holiness is greater than man and is separate from man. God alone is holy. John Miley clearly understood this when he stated, "In the deepest, divinest sense, God only is holy."[27]

Immanent Holiness

It is overwhelming and almost incomprehensible to see that God who is holy in His nature and who transcends man (and all His creation) in His holiness also condescends to dwell with man. Scripture teaches this truth mainly in Isaiah in the Old Testament, although it can be supported with passages such as Psalm 24:4 ff. God says that He dwells "with him also that is of a contrite and humble spirit" (Isa. 57:15). Jaeggli states the case aptly: "The Holy One of Israel is distinctively great in the perfection of His character and in His separation from sin, yet He also is intimately close to His people."[28]

This relationship develops on the basis of man's humility and repentance. When man sees his sinfulness in the light of God's holiness and turns to God, then God revives him. Isaiah 58 promises the same restoration to Israel when the nation forsakes sin and turns to the Lord.

Grasping this truth brings a new understanding of salvation in the New Testament. Paul declares: "But of him are ye in Christ Jesus, who of God is made unto us wisdom, and righteousness, and sanctification, and redemption" (I Cor. 1:30). Scripture provides wisdom for man, which enables him to turn to Christ in faith (see II Tim. 3:14-15). In salvation God also gives man justification, redemption, and sanctification, or holiness. Holiness is a part of God's gift of salvation! William Burt Pope thrills the soul with a statement that summarizes the Scripture's teaching on this point: "We should not, however, do justice to this attribute were we not to point out that it is revealed towards men only through an economy of grace which renders it possible that sinners, trembling before the Holy God, may become partakers of His holiness."[29]

This fact is clearly stated in a number of passages (I Cor. 6:11; Heb. 2:11; 10:10, 14; 13:12). This powerful doctrinal truth is the foundation upon which the believer can live in an imitation of God's holiness. God not only is intrinsically holy and greater than man in His holiness, but also in His holiness He comes to man through Christ to save him.

Henry Thiessen summarizes this fact of a chasm between God and man and the way God has provided to bridge it: "First, there is a chasm between God and the sinner. Secondly, that man must approach God through the merits of another. Thirdly, we should approach God with reverence and godly fear" (Heb. 12:28).[30]

God has revealed His holiness in Christ for the purpose of saving sinful men. The reason that sinners can have eternal life and fellowship with God is because God has given righteousness and holiness to men in the person of Christ. If you have never trusted Christ to save you, I have the privilege to tell you that if you will receive Him (John 1:11-12) you can know what it means to be justified before God. In Christ you will have fellowship with the holy God and the power to imitate His holiness in your daily life.

Man's Response to God's Holiness

The holiness of God demands specific responses from men, and Scripture enunciates these proper responses to the Holy God.

Penitence

When God intervened in Isaiah's life and confronted the prophet with His holiness, Isaiah acknowledged his own sinfulness (Isa. 6:5). His confession of sin resulted in God's gracious cleansing (Isa. 6:6). Because Isaiah responded to the transcendent holiness of God in repentance, he experienced the immanent holiness of God in cleansing.

After declaring His intrinsic and transcendent holiness, God assures humble and contrite men that He dwells with them (Isa. 57:15). We cannot see the holiness of God without seeing our own sinfulness. That should bring us to our knees in repentance before God.

Joy

When David brought the Ark to Jerusalem he alluded to God's holiness. He sang and instructed the people: "Glory ye in his holy name: let the heart of them rejoice that seek the Lord" (I Chron. 16:10). People who have a right relationship with God can rejoice in His holiness.

Worship

In his song of rejoicing David further instructed the people: "Give unto the Lord the glory due unto his name: bring an offering, and come before him: worship the Lord in the beauty of holiness" (I Chron. 16:29). Man responds to God's holiness in worship. He glorifies God by worshiping the beauty, or glory, of holiness. This truth is taught in several Old Testament passages (II Chron. 20:21; Pss. 29:2; 96:9). Praise of the holy God is part of worship.

Gratitude

David's song reveals that he was thankful to the holy God because He delivered the nation (I Chron. 16:35). The holiness of God excites thankfulness in the hearts of His people (Pss. 30:4; 97:12).

Imitation

God's holiness demands that His people imitate that holiness, for His holiness is the foundation of holy conduct in men. Holiness in ceremonial practice, abstaining from sin, and the practice of moral virtue are all grounded upon the fact that God is holy (Lev. 11:44; 19:2; 20:7, 26). This truth carries over to the New Testament and is the basis for holy living in the Christian's life (I Pet. 1:15-16).

Conclusion

It is apparent that separation is inherent in the meaning of the word *holiness* in the Old Testament. It is also apparent that separation is part of the meaning of the words for holiness in the New Testament.

The Scriptures declare that God is holy. God's holiness can, according to Isaiah 57:15, be divided into three aspects. God is holy intrinsically; that is, His character is holy. In His holiness God transcends all of His creation. He is glorious in His holiness. He is to be worshiped in the beauty, or glory, of His holiness. He is greater than the creation, and is separate from the creation and its sin. God is also immanent in His holiness. He dwells with contrite men and has provided His holiness as well as His wisdom, righteousness, and redemption for them by faith in Jesus.

The holiness of God should produce willing response to Him by the men whom He created. Penitence for sin will produce joy, worship, gratitude, and a passion to be like Him—to imitate His holiness. This penitence for sin before a holy God is also the key to revival. Against the modern-day inclination to rationalize and justify sinful conduct, God calls men to humble themselves and be contrite before Him. That spirit of humility and repentance brings God's gracious work of revival, which is desperately needed today.

We cannot pass this point without a plea to those who have joined in Harold John Ockenga's "repudiation of separatism."[31] Although many professing Christians have accepted this repudiation, it is a matter of utmost seriousness. We can speak neither lightly nor irreverently, but Scripture teaches that "God is a separatist."[32] This chapter lays a foundation for this claim; future chapters will build on that foundation a case for that claim. To repudiate separatism is to repudiate not a human philosophy but a teaching of revealed Scripture. That teaching is rooted deeply in the disciplines of exegetical and systematic theology. To repudiate separatism is to challenge the authority of inspired, inerrant Scripture. Those who have repudiated this teaching must reconsider their position. Men are imperfect and fallible. The man who embraces separatism may not always be right in the way he wages his battle, but the truth for which he stands is right; and it is right because it is divine, revealed truth.

Notes

[1] Samuel P. Tregelles, *Gesenius' Hebrew and Chaldee Lexicon to the Old Testament Scriptures* (Grand Rapids: Eerdmans, n.d.), p. 725.

[2] Ibid.

[3] Francis Brown, S. R. Driver, and Charles A. Briggs, *A Hebrew and English Lexicon of the Old Testament* (Oxford: Clarendon Press, 1979), p. 871.

[4] Ludwig Koehler and Walter Baumgartner, *Lexicon In Veteris Testamenti Libros* (Grand Rapids: Eerdmans, 1951), pp. 825-27.

[5] Louis Berkhof, *Systematic Theology* (Grand Rapids: Eerdmans, 1941), p. 73.

[6] Koehler and Baumgartner, p. 825.

[7] Julius Fuerst, *A Hebrew and Chaldee Lexicon to the Old Testament* (London: Williams and Norgate, 1871), p. 1221.

[8] For a detailed discussion of the meaning and usages of the Old Testament and New Testament words for holiness, see Appendix A, pp. 105-15.

[9] W. E. Vine, *Vine's Expository Dictionary of New Testament Words* (McLean: MacDonald Publishing Company, n.d.), pp. 565-67.

[10] Robert Baker Girdlestone, *Synonyms of the Old Testament* (Reprint ed., Grand Rapids: Eerdmans, 1976), p. 179.

[11] Richard Chenevix Trench, *Synonyms of the New Testament* (Grand Rapids: Eerdmans, 1963), p. 331.

[12] See Appendix I.

[13] Charles C. Ryrie, *Basic Theology* (Wheaton: Victor Books, 1986), p. 38.

[14] Augustus Hopkins Strong, *Systematic Theology* (Valley Forge, Pa.: Judson Press, 1907), p. 268.

[15] George Christian Knapp, *Lectures on Christian Theology* (Philadelphia: J.W. Moore, 1851), p. 116.

[16] Thomas Watson, *A Body of Divinity* (Reprint ed., London: Banner of Truth Trust, 1970), p. 83.

[17] William G. T. Shedd, *Dogmatic Theology* (Grand Rapids: Zondervan, n.d.), 1:362.

[18] Carl E. Armerding, "Habakkuk," Frank E. Gaebelein, ed., *The Expositor's Bible Commentary* (Grand Rapids: Zondervan, 1985), 7:505.

[19] Louis Goldberg, "חלל," R. Laird Harris, ed. *Theological Wordbook of the Old Testament* (Chicago: Moody Press, 1980), 1:304.

[20]John Randolph Jaeggli, "An Historical-Theological Analysis of the Holy One of Israel in Isaiah Forty Through Sixty-Six" (Ph.D. Dissertation, Bob Jones University, 1987), p. 155.

[21]Strong, p. 273.

[22]Watson, p. 83.

[23]The glory of God is a subject all its own, but one which must be comprehended. Thomas L. Zempel, "A Biblical Approach To Understanding the Physical Handicap of Down's Syndrome" (D.Min. Project, Westminster Theological Seminary, 1990), pp. 16-19, shows that the Old Testament meaning of *glory* is "heavy" or "weighty." Applied to a person it speaks of "substance," thus the honor or dignity which gives a person importance. Therefore, God's glory is His honor, or His worth. Beyond Zempel's study, there are several salient facts to note: (1) God's glory is the manifestation of His presence with men. This presence is usually revealed in Scripture by a brilliant light (see Exod. 24:16-17; 33:18-23; 34:29-35; II Chron. 7:1-3; Luke 2:9; I Tim. 6:16; Rev. 21:3, 23). (2) God's glory is the honor, or praise that is due His name (Isa. 42:8). (3) Man's sinfulness is directly related to his failure to glorify his Creator (Rom. 1:21, 24). (4) God revealed His glory in the incarnation of Christ (John 1:14; Heb. 1:1-3). (5) The glory of God, revealed in Christ, comes through the gospel to save men (II Cor. 4:3-6). (6) Redeemed man is to live for the glory of God (Matt. 5:16; I Cor. 10:31; I Pet. 4:11). (7) Eternal glory awaits the redeemed (II Cor. 4:17).

[24]Girdlestone, p. 178.

[25]J. Stanley Chestnut, *The Old Testament Understanding of God* (Philadelphia: Westminster Press, 1968), p. 133.

[26]Ibid.

[27]John Miley, *Systematic Theology* (New York: Eaton and Mains, 1892), 1:199.

[28]Jaeggli, p. 46.

[29]William Burt Pope, *A Compendium of Christian Theology* (New York: Phillips and Hunt, n.d.), 1:334.

[30]Henry C. Thiessen, *Lectures in Systematic Theology* (Grand Rapids: Eerdmans, 1949), p. 124.

[31]Lindsell, p. 11.

[32]Ernest Pickering, *Biblical Separation: The Struggle For A Pure Church* (Schaumburg: Regular Baptist Press, 1979), p. 173.

2

PERSONAL SEPARATION

Children are born imitators. As infants they watch the movements of people's mouths, and over a period of months they learn to imitate those movements and talk. Little girls dress up in mother's clothes, shoes, makeup, and accessories. They also want to help mother cook. A little boy wants to dress like his dad and go where he goes. He subconsciously learns to imitate father's gait as he walks. All of this may be humorous to observe, but it is a major way that children learn in their early years.

When I was in my first pastorate, we had a church softball team, and I enjoyed playing with the other fellows. One day my son Jimmy, who was four at the time, "borrowed" my ball glove for a while. When he had finished playing with it he left it in the yard, and while it was there a heavy rainstorm came. My glove was ruined! I bought a new one and warned him that if he played with it, I would spank him. A few days later I drove into the driveway of our home and found Jimmy playing with my glove in the yard. What I saw was so funny I did not have the heart to keep my word and spank him.

We lived west of Chicago and were close enough to the city to get the big league baseball games on television. Jimmy had been watching a game when one of the teams brought in a relief pitcher. While the new man was warming up, the television crew showed him in slow motion. Jimmy had watched the slow motion replay of his delivery, and was in the yard, duplicating a big league delivery in slow motion. He "came set," looked over his left shoulder toward first base, leaned back on his right leg, lifted his left leg a few inches off the ground, moved forward, and delivered the ball perfectly to home plate. The sight broke me up, as you can imagine. He had been watching the big league pitcher and had learned to imitate him perfectly.

The New Testament applies this principle of imitation to the learning and growing process in the life of a Christian. Paul recounts that the Thessalonian believers, after they were saved, became "followers" of him, and then of the Lord (I Thess. 1:6). The word which the Holy Spirit uses for followers is the word μιμητής (*mimētēs*), which means "imitator."[1] From that same word our English language gets the words *mime, mimic, mimeograph,* and *imitate*. The Thessalonians saw and imitated Paul's Christ-like life, and, because Paul imitated Christ, the Thessalonian believers also learned to imitate Christ Himself. Paul intended for this to happen in the lives of his converts. He said, "Imitate me, just as I also imitate Christ."[2] This illustration applies specifically to the lifestyle of the Christian, to the subject of personal separation, and to its relationship to God's holiness. Peter exhorts believers, "As obedient children, not fashioning yourselves according to the former lusts in your ignorance: but as he which hath called you is holy, so be ye holy in all manner of conversation; because it is written, Be ye holy; for I am holy. And if ye call on the Father, who without respect of persons judgeth according to every man's work, pass the time of your sojourning here in fear" (I Pet. 1:14-17).

The fact that the Christian has been born again (I Pet. 1:3) forms the foundation of Peter's argument in these verses. Natural birth produces a desire in children to be like their parents. The new birth plants within the child of God a desire to be like his heavenly Father.

In I Peter 1:14 Peter uses a word which describes the pattern of the Christian's life. He instructs Christians "as obedient children, not fashioning yourselves according to the former lusts." The word which is translated "fashioning" is the participle form of the word συσχηματίζω (*suschēmatizō*) which means "to form or mold after something . . . be formed like, be conformed to, be guided by."[3] This word is the source of the English word *schema* which means "a diagram, plan, or scheme; an abstract or conceptual outline, or plan, as of doctrines or a process."[4] *Schematic* is the common term for a diagram which shows the flow of electricity through a circuit.

Scripture is saying that obedient children of God are not to form or mold their lives according to the sinful lusts which ruled them before their salvation. A new pattern, or "schematic," should form their manner of life as people who have been born again. That new mold which forms the lifestyle of the believer is the holiness of God. "As he which hath called you is holy, so be ye holy in all manner of conversation" (I Pet. 1:15).

Peter concludes his exhortation with another strong reference to the father-child relationship between God and Christians. He states: "And if Father ye yourselves call upon, the one impartially judging according to every one's work, in fear live ye[5] your sojourn time" (I Pet. 1:17; author's literal translation). Kenneth Wuest elaborates: "The idea in the Greek is 'in view of the fact that you call on as Father.' That is, they recognized God as their Father since they had been brought into the family of God in salvation."[6] Charles R. Erdman points out that this verse is one of two reasons given for obeying the command to holiness. God is "just, and can allow no sin in his children; therefore, we should spend the brief time of our 'sojourning' here . . . 'in reverence and holy awe.' "[7] The holy God is the one the believer calls upon as his Father. Therefore he is commanded to live in reverence, or the fear of God during his time on earth. J.N.D. Kelly distills the ideas of verses fourteen and seventeen: "The writer's point is that, since the God whom his readers address as Father is to be their judge, they would be wise to have a healthy dread of His judgment and shape their behavior accordingly."[8]

The Christian has been born again (I Pet. 1:3). As an obedient child of God, his lifestyle is not to be formed according to his old, sinful passions (I Pet. 1:14), but according to the pattern of the holiness of God (I Pet. 1:15-16). Since the believer calls God his Father, he is to live according to this pattern in reverence for the one who will judge his work.

We have clearly seen that God's holiness demands specific responses from man. Repentance, worship, praise, joy, and thanksgiving are proper responses to God's holiness. The final response by men to God's holiness is the one most emphasized in Scripture. Men should respond to God's holiness with a desire to be like Him; that is, to imitate His holiness. Personal separation is nothing else but the believer's rejection of his old sinful passions and his imitation of God's holiness in his lifestyle.

Our first chapter demonstrated that the idea of separation forms an integral part of the concept of holiness. In this chapter we propose to demonstrate that the Christian's practice of separation from sin flows from God's holiness. The Holy God gives His holiness to men through Christ and calls upon the believer to imitate His holiness in his lifestyle.

The Old Testament Principle of Holiness

God's Holiness and Human Conduct

The truth that God calls His people to imitate His holiness becomes abundantly clear as the Old Testament teaching on holiness unfolds. We have seen that God's holiness determines the standard of human conduct. Leviticus 19 and 20 delineates both personal and religious practices. Some personal practices are commanded and others are forbidden. The two chapters begin and end with affirmations of God's holiness (Lev. 19:2; 20:26). The statements "I am the Lord" or "I am the Lord your God" are repeated nineteen times (Lev. 19:3, 4, 10, 12, 14, 16, 18, 25, 28, 30, 31, 32, 34, 36, 37; 20:7, 8, 24, 26). God declares that idolatry will "profane my holy name" (Lev. 20:3), and He warns them against witchcraft (Lev. 20:6). The reason they are to separate themselves is His holiness: "Sanctify yourselves therefore, and be ye holy: for I am the Lord your God" (Lev. 20:7). He commands them to obey His revelation because "I am the Lord which sanctify you" (Lev. 20:8). Near the end of the chapter God forbids Israel to live as the Canaanites and again commands them to obey His Word. The reason is, again, that "I am the Lord which have separated you from other people" (Lev. 20:24).

Commanded Actions

The personal practices which God commanded include reverence for parents (Lev. 19:3), practicing righteous judgment (Lev. 19:15, 35-36), love for one's neighbor (Lev. 19:18), respect for the elderly (Lev. 19:32), and love for the stranger (Lev. 19:33-34).

Forbidden Actions

In addition to idolatry and witchcraft, God forbids other personal practices, including stealing, false dealing, and lying (Lev. 19:11), defrauding a neighbor (Lev. 19:13), discrimination against the handicapped (Lev. 19:14), talebearing (Lev. 19:16), hatred (Lev. 19:17), bearing a grudge (Lev. 19:18), prostitution (Lev. 19:29), cursing one's parents (Lev. 20:9), adultery (Lev. 20:10-12), homosexual practice (Lev. 20:13), bestiality (Lev. 20:15-16), and other deviant sexual conduct (Lev. 20:14, 17-21).

One can hardly avoid concluding that obedience to the positive actions and the forsaking of the forbidden practices constitutes a reflection of the desires of the holy God in the lives of His people. The principle is established that God's people by obedience to Him reflect His holiness in their conduct. C. D. Ginsburg, noting the repeated declarations of God's holiness in Leviticus 19, clearly summarizes the issue: "It is this solemn formula which links together the various injunctions in the chapter before us. As the Lord who is their God is Himself holy, they who are his people must also be holy . . . or, in other words, your nearness to God not only demands that your conduct should not be in contradiction to His holy nature, but that your life should bear the impress and reflect the image of God."[9] God's purpose for His people is that they be holy as He is holy (Lev. 19:2; 20:7, 26).

God's Holiness and His Fear

The concept of the fear of God is tied to the concept of the holiness of God and to the practice of personal separation. The statement "The fear of the Lord is the beginning of wisdom; and the knowledge of the holy is understanding" (Prov. 9:10) directly connects the fear of God with the holiness of God. The fear of God appears predominately in the Old Testament, although this truth is also taught in the New Testament.[10]

The fear of God connects to the practice of personal separation in Leviticus 19. Verses 14 and 32 carry the reminder of God's holiness with the statement "I am the Lord" followed by the command that men fear God. The same relationship exists in Leviticus 25:17. The Old Testament establishes the fact that God's holiness is the standard for human conduct, and that men who fear God will learn holiness and forsake evil.

The Possibility of Holiness

The possibility that the believer can imitate God's holiness, or live a life of personal separation to God from sin, lies in the finished work of Jesus Christ on the cross. Apart from salvation through Him, there is no possibility of forsaking sin, imitating God's holiness, or having victory over sin. This is that part of the doctrine of salvation which is commonly identified as "sanctification."

Paul describes his desire to do good, his frustration with ever-present sin, and the war he experiences within himself (Rom. 7:21-23). He then describes the only hope for victory and deliverance: "O wretched man that I am! Who shall deliver me from the body of this death? I thank God through Jesus Christ our Lord. So then with the mind I myself serve the law of God; but with the flesh the law of sin" (Rom. 7:24-25). Paul not only reposes his hope in Christ, but he also clearly declares that the work of Christ provides the believer with the potential for a life of holiness, or personal separation. This is God's work of sanctification for the believer.

Christ's Death and Holiness

Scripture teaches that Christ died on the cross in order to make peace, or reconcile all things to Himself (Col. 1:20). Men who are alienated from God by their sin, are, when they receive Christ as their Savior, reconciled to Him in this present life. They now have peace and fellowship with God. The ultimate purpose of Christ for them is "in the body of his flesh through death, to present you holy and unblameable and unreproveable in his sight" (Col. 1:22). The believer will be presented to God "holy" and "blameless,"[11] "as those who cannot even be called to account for sin."[12]

Scripture teaches in addition that sanctification is provided by the work of Christ on the cross. "By the which will we are sanctified through the offering of the body of Jesus Christ once for all. . . . For by one offering he hath perfected for ever them that are sanctified" (Heb. 10:10, 14). Jesus provided this eternal work of sanctification for the believer by His one-time death. Scripture further teaches that this sanctification was accomplished through the shedding of Christ's blood (Heb. 13:12). Sanctification, or holiness, will be completed when the believer stands "in his sight" (Col. 1:22), or "in the presence of" God.[13] More will be said about this in coming pages.

We must take the time to deal with the issue of how sanctification, or holiness, is received. Scripture clearly teaches that sanctification, or holiness, was provided by Christ for men when He died on the cross as their substitute. Scripture is equally clear that holiness is received as a part of salvation, by faith in Christ. Paul remembered his commission from Christ when he stood before Agrippa. He said that Christ sent him "to open their eyes, and to turn them from darkness to light, and from the power of Satan unto God, that they may receive forgiveness of sins, and inheritance among them which are sanctified by faith that is in me" (Acts 26:18).

For an individual to have the blessings of salvation, one of which is the inheritance among the sanctified, he must trust the Lord Jesus Christ for salvation. As has been previously shown, the blessings of wisdom, righteousness, sanctification, and redemption are given to men by God in Christ Jesus (I Cor. 1:30). In order to be delivered from sin and to have the power to live in imitation of God's holiness, one must be saved by simple faith in Christ.

Justification and Holiness

The Bible teaches that holiness in the life of the believer is the result of the believer's justification by faith in Christ. Romans 3:21–5:21 sets forth the truth of justification by faith. When a sinful man trusts Christ, God imputes His righteousness to that sinful man and declares him righteous (Rom. 3:21-26). By faith in Christ the believer is identified with Christ in His death and in His resurrection (Rom. 6:3-4). Because of the Christian's union with Christ, the body of sin has been destroyed. The verb used, καταργέω (*katargeō*), means "to make ineffective, powerless, idle."[14] The believer therefore no longer needs to serve sin but has been freed from sin (Rom. 6:6-7). He now is to yield himself to God and his "members as instruments of righteousness unto God" (Rom. 6:13). As a servant of righteousness the result, or fruit, in his life is twice declared to be holiness (Rom. 6:19, 22). Holiness in life is the result of the imputed righteousness of God to the believer in Christ.

Paul teaches the same truth to the Corinthian Christians. He begins by describing the unrighteous (I Cor. 6:9). They will not inherit the kingdom of God. He characterizes them as "fornicators," "idolaters," "adulterers," "effeminate,"[15] "abusers of themselves with mankind,"[16] "thieves," "covetous," "drunkards," "revilers,"[17]

27

and "extortioners"[18] (I Cor. 6:9-10). He then describes the drama of their conversion by saying, "And such were some of you: but ye are washed, but ye are sanctified, ye are justified in the name of the Lord Jesus, and by the Spirit of our God" (I Cor. 6:11). God reaches down to men who practice the most horrendous sins and saves them. By faith in Christ, men are washed, sanctified, and justified. Sanctification, that is holiness—and the potential for holy living, is the result of justification by faith.

Righteousness and Holiness

Because holiness is made possible through the Christian's justification by faith, righteousness and holiness are linked together several times in the New Testament. It only stands to reason that holiness will be seen as the result of righteousness. If justification provides the potential for holiness at salvation (Rom. 6; I Cor. 6), then holiness will be the outworking of righteousness in daily living. Ephesians 4:17–5:21 will be examined in detail later in this chapter. At this point it should be noted that the theme of righteousness and holiness are important in the passage. The Scripture states, "And that ye put on the new man, which after God is created in righteousness and true holiness" (Eph. 4:24). The word order puts righteousness ahead of holiness. The conclusion is that God's righteousness produces holiness in the conduct of the believer's life. It is important to note that the word for holiness in this passage is from the family of ὅσιος (hosios) rather than ἅγιος (hagios). As previously noted, the emphasis of ὅσιος is on piety. The concrete idea of holiness is in the fabric of the passage (see Eph. 4:30; 5:3, 18). The point of Ephesians 4:24 is that the righteousness of God produces the new man. This new, or regenerated, man, empowered by the Holy Spirit who dwells in his body, gives evidence of true piety in his life. This is a reflection of the holiness of God.

Another major passage which demonstrates the relationship between righteousness and holiness is Revelation 22:11. Unrighteousness produces filthiness in lifestyle, and righteousness produces holiness of life.

Positional Holiness

Because holy living is made possible by the finished work of Christ, the Bible teaches that the believer is viewed by God as having been sanctified at the time of his salvation. His position is that of a "saint" or "holy one."

Called Saints

Several passages of Scripture describe the positional holiness of the believer before God by simply calling Christians "saints." Some of the passages which so describe believers are Romans 1:7; I Corinthians 1:2; II Corinthians 1:1; Ephesians 1:1; Philippians 1:1; and Colossians 1:2. The believers are "sanctified in Christ Jesus, called to be saints" (I Cor. 1:2).

Called Holy

There are several seemingly stronger indications of the position the Christian occupies before the Lord. In several places Christians are addressed as being "holy." They are called "holy and beloved" (Col. 3:12); "holy brethren" (I Thess. 5:27; Heb. 3:1); "an holy priesthood" (I Pet. 2:5); and "an holy nation" (I Pet. 2:9).

Holiness and Evangelism

A crucial truth must be noted at this point. The believer is sanctified by the work of Christ on the cross; he stands before God as a "saint" and a "holy one." Upon the basis of his standing before God it is possible for him to live a holy life. It must be said in this context that *separation is not isolation!* God's purpose for the separated Christian life, or holy lifestyle, is rather for the believer to have an effective, powerful witness in the world. The Christian's lifestyle will be different than it was when he lived according to the "former lusts" (I Pet. 1:14). There will be a radical change in the pattern of his life, and his life will be modeled after the holiness of God (I Pet. 1:15-16). Believers are a "holy nation" whose purpose is to "shew forth the praises of him who hath called you out of darkness into his marvellous light" (I Pet. 2:9). The purpose of holy living is to show lost men the difference that Christ makes in an individual's life. Christians are not to be isolated from the world, but rather to live holy lives in the world.

The Lord Jesus stated this principle in His prayer of John 17. He declared that His disciples are "not of the world" (John 17:14). He then prayed, not that the Father would take them out of the world, but that He would "keep them from the evil" (John 17:15). He prayed for their sanctification through the word (John 17:17), and for those "which shall believe on me through their word" (John 17:20). God intends that the difference in the believer's life while he is in the world will result in others believing on Christ. Personal separation is a complement to soulwinning and evangelism.

The Practice of Holiness

Scripture goes beyond teaching the positional holiness of the Christian to declare that the imitation of God's holiness should be the practice of the believer's life.

Necessity of Holiness

The necessity of holiness is seen in the fact that it is God's will for the believer and the fact that it is a prerequisite for Christian service.

God's Will for the Believer

Scripture clearly states that the practical imitation of God's holiness by the believer is the will of God. Paul states, "For this is the will of God, even your sanctification, that ye should abstain from fornication" (I Thess. 4:3). He then goes on to say: "For God hath not called us to uncleanness, but unto holiness" (I Thess. 4:7). Sanctification, or a holy lifestyle, is manifestly the will of God. In this instance the evidence of that holy lifestyle is moral purity. Indeed, when God devised the plan of salvation before the creation of the world, His purpose for the believer was a "holy calling" (II Tim. 1:9).

Prerequisite for Service

Holiness in lifestyle is the beginning of Christian service. Romans 12:1 states, "I beseech you therefore, brethren, by the mercies of God, that ye present your bodies a living sacrifice, holy, acceptable unto God, which is your reasonable service." Service does not begin for the Christian with a call to a particular work. Rather, it begins when the Christian presents his body to God. The condition in which God wants the body is "holy," and that presentation of the body to God is the beginning of Christian service. Service for God begins with holiness of life.

Means of Holiness

Scripture declares that God uses several means to accomplish holiness in the believer's life.

Scripture

God's Word is one of the instruments which God uses to enable the believer to imitate His holiness. In His prayer for believers in John 17:17, 19, Jesus said, "Sanctify them through thy truth: Thy word is truth. . . . And for their sakes I sanctify myself, that they also might be sanctified through the truth." Earlier He declared that believers are cleansed by His Word (John 15:3). This passage illustrates the truth that God uses His Word to conform believers to His holiness. Note again that this passage emphasizes that separation is not isolation but that God uses a Christian's holy life along with His Word to bring sinners to faith in Christ.

God's Spirit

The Holy Spirit is directly linked with the believer's imitation of God's holiness and his separation from sinful practices. In the midst of a long list of sins which the believer is commanded to abandon, he is told "And grieve not the Holy Spirit of God" (Eph. 4:30). At the conclusion of that passage the believer is instructed to "be filled with the Spirit" (Eph. 5:18).[19] When the believer tolerates sin in his life, he grieves the Holy Spirit and hinders His work in his life. When the Spirit fills or controls the believer, then the believer will evidence holiness, or piety of life (Eph. 4:24). H.C.G. Moule points out that this kind of lifestyle is "possible only (if it is to be a reality) in the power of the eternal Spirit."[20] Scripture also teaches that the believer, seeing God's glory in the Word, is changed by the Spirit into the image of God's glory (II Cor. 3:18).

Discipline

Another of God's means for producing holiness is the chastening which God periodically brings into our lives. The author of Hebrews illustrates the believer's relationship to God with the father-child relationship: "For they [human fathers] verily for a few days chastened us after their own pleasure; but he for our profit, that we might be partakers of his holiness" (Heb. 12:10). The next verse declares that this correction "yieldeth the peaceable fruit of righteousness" in the disciplined believer's life (Heb. 12:11).[21]

Progressive Nature of Holiness

It is clear that the believer's position before God is that of a "holy one." It is also clear that holiness in lifestyle is a progressive work of God in the life of the child of God. Holiness in lifestyle is God's will and is a prerequisite for service. It develops as the Christian abides in the Word of God, surrenders to the control of the Spirit of God, and is exercised by divine chastening. As he yields to these divine influences, the practice of holiness is progressively produced in his life. He is progressively changed into the image of the Lord Jesus Christ (II Cor. 3:17-18). Charles Hodge crystallizes the truth: "Sanctification, therefore, consists in two things: first, the renouncing more and more of the principles of evil still infecting our nature, and destroying their power; and secondly, the growth of the principle of spiritual life until it controls the thoughts, feelings, and acts, and brings the soul into conformity to the image of Christ."[22]

Manifestation of Holiness

As we have clearly seen from Scripture, the holiness of God changes the lifestyle and daily life of the Christian. After this principle is established, a critical question remains: How does the principle that holiness affects the believer's lifestyle translate into everyday action? Several New Testament passages speak to Christians about specific actions which should characterize their lives, passages such as Galatians 5:16-26, Ephesians 4:17–5:18, and Colossians 3:1-11. The Ephesians passage, which ties the holiness of God to these actions and is the most extensive of the three, will be considered in particular. This section also considers Philippians 4:8 on the relationship of holiness to a believer's thoughts.

It must be noted at the outset that the theme of holiness permeates this passage. The believer is commanded to live in contrast to the normal lifestyle of the Gentile world (Eph. 4:17). The mark of this different lifestyle is "righteousness and true holiness" (Eph. 4:24). As previously noted, the word for holiness conveys the idea of "piety." A. Skevington Wood defines it as "free from contamination."[23] The righteousness of God will produce the fruit of holiness (Rom. 6:19, 22) and a lifestyle free from the corruption of sin—a lifestyle of piety (Eph. 4:24). This is in direct contrast to the old nature which is corrupt (Eph. 4:22) and is, as John Eadie says, "becoming more corrupt."[24]

The Bible also presents holiness as the result of the Holy Spirit's work in the Christian life. He creates the "new man," or regenerates the believer (Eph. 4:24). Sin grieves the Spirit (Eph. 4:30). The Holy Spirit gives goodness, righteousness, and truth in the believer's life as His fruit (Eph. 5:9). The Spirit-filled believer has victory over sin (Eph. 5:18).

This key passage reveals a further characteristic of holiness. The believer is to repudiate sin "as becometh saints" (Eph. 5:3). The practice of holiness is possible in the Christian's life because of his holy position before God.

Sin Abhorred

Paul declares that believers who are positionally holy, indwelt and filled by the Holy Spirit, will abhor sin. He states that they are to "walk not as other Gentiles walk" (Eph. 4:17); "put off . . . the old man" (v. 22) and "put on the new man" (v. 24). He further lists a whole series of sins which Christians are to remove from their lives: lasciviousness (4:19),[25] all uncleanness (4:19),[26] greediness (translated "covetousness" and "covetous" in 5:3, 5), lying (4:25), anger (4:26, 31),[27] wrath (4:26, 31),[28] stealing (4:28), corrupt communication (4:29),[29] bitterness (4:31), clamor,[30] evil speaking (4:31),[31] malice (4:31),[32] fornication (5:3),[33] filthiness (5:3),[34] foolish talking, and jesting (5:4).[35] He goes on to speak of the whoremonger, the unclean man, and the covetous man (5:5).

Several facts stand out as this passage is analyzed. First, the intensity of the passage is readily apparent. Fornication is named twice, the whoremonger once, and immorality is referred to in an oblique manner a fourth time (4:19). Uncleanness is named twice and filthiness is added to it. Covetousness is named three times. The manner of a Christian's speech is dealt with four times. Paul is on a rampage against sin.

Second, sins of the heart or spirit are dealt with as much as overt, committed acts. Passionate desire, bitterness, and malicious attitudes towards others are proscribed and are described as being contrary to God's holiness.

Third, a lifestyle which rejects the aforementioned sins is becoming of the believer whose position before God is a "saint" or "holy one" (5:3). This godly lifestyle will be produced by the Spirit who fills the believer's life (5:18) and is the mark of true holiness or piety of life (4:24).

Virtue Pursued

To leave this passage at this point would be to tell only half of the story. Scripture demands that the believer, imitating the holiness of God, forsake sin; but it also commands the believer to develop certain virtues in his life. These positive actions and attitudes reflect the holiness of God in the believer's life as much as the absence of forbidden sin does. The Christian is instructed to speak the truth in love (4:15, 25). He is told to deal promptly with anger so that he will not "give place to the devil" in his life (4:26-27). William Hendricksen explains that Satan is capable of "changing our indignation . . . into a grievance, a grudge, a nursing of wrath, an unwillingness to forgive."[36] The Christian is to work for a living in order to be able to give (4:28) and to speak in such a way to build up those whom he addresses (4:29). The believer is to be characterized by a kind, tenderhearted, forgiving spirit (4:32), and his lifestyle is to be marked by love (5:2). Further, his life is to be characterized by light (5:8).[37] He is to exhibit the fruit of the Holy Spirit in his life (5:9).

Purified in Thought

Scripture also relates the thought life of the believer to the concept of holiness. Paul says, "Finally, brethren, whatsoever things are true, whatsoever things are honest, whatsoever things are just, whatsoever things are pure, whatsoever things are lovely, whatsoever things are of a good report; if there be any virtue, and if there be any praise, think on these things" (Phil. 4:8).

The believer is to discipline his thoughts to meet this eightfold standard. One of the criteria for the believer's thought life is the standard of purity. The word for "pure" (ἁγνός; *hagnos*), as noted in Chapter One, is related to the word for holiness. Homer A. Kent states that the word "emphasizes moral purity and includes in some contexts the more restricted sense of 'chaste.' "[38] It must be understood that holiness in the lifestyle of the Christian will affect the thoughts as well as the spirit and outward conduct.

The Perfection of Holiness

The believer's sanctification will be completed in heaven. When Christ returns, the believer will be perfected in holiness. God's purpose for the Christian is clear in this regard. Paul states, "To the end he may stablish your hearts unblameable in holiness before God, even our Father, at the coming of our Lord Jesus Christ with all his saints" (I Thess. 3:13). He sees both their present sanctification and its completion at the return of Christ: "And the very God of peace sanctify you wholly; and I pray God your whole spirit and soul and body be preserved blameless unto the coming of our Lord Jesus Christ" (I Thess. 5:23).

The apostle states that God's purpose for believers is that they "should be holy and without blame before him in love" (Eph. 1:4). Eadie demonstrates that Paul has eternity in mind: "The eternal purpose not only pardons, but also sanctifies, absolves in order to renew, and purifies in order to bestow perfection. It is the uniform teaching of Paul that holiness is the end of our election, our calling, our pardon and acceptance."[39] In other passages (I Cor. 3:17; Eph. 2:21; 5:27), Scripture also teaches that the church will be perfected in holiness in eternity.

In short, holiness in the believer is prospective. It will be accomplished when the believer is perfected in the likeness of Christ (I John 3:2-3).

The Problem of Holiness

In partial answer to the earlier question of how holiness affects the believer's lifestyle, the principle of holiness translates into every action. Scripture identifies specific conduct which is contrary to God's holiness and must be put off. It also describes actions and attitudes which reflect God's holiness and must be put on. Whenever Scripture prohibits an attitude or action, a believer is to forsake it. Whenever Scripture commands an attitude or action, a believer is to obey it. These actions and attitudes are either contrary to or reflective of the holiness of God.

Yet the issue of personal separation is not completely resolved. The question which remains is: How does the believer set a standard of conduct for actions to which Scripture does not specifically speak? This would include such issues as dress standards, movie attendance, the use of tobacco and drugs, music standards, and other matters. The Christian must determine these matters in his own mind and heart.

Legalism

Twentieth-century Christianity has traditionally taken a conservative stance on these and other issues. Until the last several years Hollywood movies, the modern dance, the use of alcohol, and music which was worldly in its influence were almost universally rejected. This situation has changed dramatically over the last several years. There is intense debate in many quarters over these and other issues. The term *legalism* has come into popular use as this debate has progressed. Kurt DeHaan defines the term: "In the biblical sense, the term *legalism* describes human attempts to gain salvation and/or spiritual maturity through self-help and conformity to a list of religious laws. A person who sees legalism as a way of salvation and continuing acceptance by God is called a legalist."[40] This study will deal only with the area of legalism that pertains to Christian lifestyle and spirituality.[41]

This issue merits attention because it is related to what the Bible teaches about the believer's lifestyle and to the issue of holiness that is so prominent in the biblical frame of reference. Douglas McLachlan assesses the situation that has developed: "It is critical that we deal with this matter, for there is a shift far too much to the 'left' in much of modern fundamentalism—a reactionary move from those in the present generation who would like to make war with their brethren from the past generation. I, for one, will have no part of any such war."[42]

DeHaan[43] and McLachlan[44] both speak of the legalist as one who makes a list or code for conduct. They say that the public perception is that conformity to the list constitutes spirituality. Charles Swindoll also concurs in this understanding of legalism when he states, "It is an obsessive conformity to an artificial standard for the purpose of exalting oneself."[45]

Responses to Legalism

We need to make several observations on the issue of legalism. When leaders attempt to set standards for institutions or churches which they lead they are frequently labeled as "legalists." Pastors who preach the biblical concept of personal separation are often subjected to the same caricature. It is clear as Ken Pulliam says, however, that "having standards is not the same as being a legalist."[46] The charge is used all too often to justify the "shift to the left" against which McLachlan wrote.

Bible Lists

The first response to the issue of legalism is that *it is always right to live by any list contained in Scripture.* The passage we looked at in Ephesians 4 and 5 is such a list. Conformity to these lists is neither wrong nor legalistic but rather simple obedience to the instructions of Scripture. DeHaan notes this fact and cites the list which Paul includes in Galatians 5:19-21.[47] Swindoll also recognizes the same truth.[48]

Standards Necessary

The second response to the issue of legalism must deal with the necessity of standards. Pulliam lists two biblical reasons for standards, namely God's holiness and "to maintain a consistent Christian testimony."[49] Parents must set standards of conduct for their children in the home. Leaders must of necessity set standards for those whom they lead in churches, Christian schools, Christian colleges, and other institutions. To fail to have standards is to invite confusion, disorder, and harm to the cause of Christ. It must be understood that some of these standards will not be scriptural per se, but leaders need to be sure that those standards reflect biblical principles. Leaders also need to communicate the message that conformity to the standards does not make a person spiritual. Yet the need for order and harmony in a ministry demands that some standards be set.

Standards Not Legalism

The third response to the charge of legalism is that the sincere pastor, college president, or other Christian leader who seeks to set standards which are consistent with the Bible and which promote godliness is not a legalist. He is nothing like the Pharisees of Jesus' day, who according to Unger

> multiplied minute precepts and distinctions to such an extent, upon the pretense of maintaining it [the law] intact, that the whole life of Israel was hemmed in and burdened on every side by instructions so numerous and trifling that the law was almost, if not wholly, lost sight of. . . . Vain and trifling questions took the place of serious inquiry into the great principles of duty; and even the most solemn truths were handled as mere matters of curious speculation or means to entrap an adversary.[50]

The pastor, leader, or parent who is concerned about the moral purity, sobriety, modesty, spiritual growth, and effective Christian service of those in his church, institution, or home is *not* a legalist when he seeks to set standards which are consistent with Scripture and which promote godliness! We cannot state this fact too emphatically.

Heart Attitude

Scripture emphasizes the importance of a right attitude of heart in the believer along with his conformity to the outward standard set by God. The father-child relationship which Peter emphasizes certainly implies an intimate relationship in which a believer desires to imitate his heavenly Father as a child desires to be like his earthly father.

In Ephesians 4 and 5 the believer's actions—telling the truth in love, giving, edifying by speech, forsaking ill will, and demonstrating tenderness of heart—all speak clearly of the believer's positive disposition toward his fellow man. The command to "walk in love" (Eph. 5:2) indicates that his walk is to reflect his attitude toward God.

Scripture does not emphasize a robot-like conformity to a list of prohibited and prescribed actions. Its emphasis rather is that a right attitude will produce positive actions which reflect the holiness of God. These actions can only be produced by the Holy Spirit in the life of the Christian who is surrendered to Him (Eph. 4:30; 5:18). *A proper attitude of heart is essential to the right practice of personal separation.*

There are other indications in Scripture that the Christian is to have a spirit which will produce a passion for holiness. Scripture instructs the believer to "follow peace with all men, and holiness, without which no man shall see the Lord" (Heb. 12:14). The believer is to "follow," that is, "pursue without hostility . . . (as one would a calling)."[51] This indicates a desire for holiness on the part of the believer. Paul teaches believers to be "perfecting holiness in the fear of God" (II Cor. 7:1). They are to seek to "fully complete"[52] holiness. Jesus will return to receive believers to Himself. The believer who looks for Christ "purifieth himself even as he is pure" (I John 3:3).

A desire to imitate the heavenly Father, genuine love for Him, tenderheartedness towards fellow believers, following holiness as a calling, seeking to perfect holiness, and an imitation of Christ whose return is imminent are all the attitudes of heart which motivate the practice of personal separation.

Spirituality is not determined by outward conformity to a prescribed standard for human conduct, whether that standard is found in Scripture or set by man. But the believer who refuses to conform to the standards of Scripture will *always* reveal the glaring lack of a right attitude toward God and His holiness. When a believer, on the other hand, develops the proper perspective toward God and His holiness, he will gladly live in conformity to the standards which God sets in His Word. Those in places of leadership need to be sure that they stress the Christian's walk with God over the standards which they find it necessary to set and enforce.

Principles to Apply

Each generation of Christians must grapple with specific activities regarding which Scripture does not speak directly. They must apply the principles of holiness in those situations. Further, the believer must determine what things are "expedient" and what things "edify" (I Cor. 10:23) in determining his actions.

Leaders must be careful not to convey the notion that conformity to standards equates with spirituality. They must preach to the hearts of their followers and depend on the Holy Spirit to produce the heart attitudes which will result in conformity to scriptural standards. Fundamentalists should maintain their resolve in holding to standards for conduct which reflect the biblical principles of holiness, but they should also think through their standards and be able to defend them with Scripture.

The application of biblical principles to present-day activities is crucial. Philippians 4:8 is unequivocal about the Christian's thoughts. Truthfulness, honesty, righteousness, and purity are among the virtues which Scripture says should characterize the believer's thought life. On the other side of the issue, Jesus taught in Matthew 15:19 that evil thoughts are the source of "murders, adulteries, fornications, thefts, false witness, blasphemies." Preachers need to apply these biblical principles in their pulpit ministries, and all Christians need to apply them in the decisions of everyday life. It staggers the imagination to think that a modern-day Christian could understand these biblical principles and then justify watching and hearing the profanity, immorality, violence, and un-biblical ethics and philosophies propounded by Hollywood enter-tainment, whether in motion pictures or on television. To feed the mind with pornography or with literature, music, and forms of entertainment that are sensual or blatantly immoral—such behavior flies in the face of any reasonable understanding of Bible principles. This is where the shift to the left of which McLachlan spoke becomes apparent.

Charles Swindoll's thinking seems to be flawed at this point. His book *The Grace Awakening* has a long section on accepting others and not imposing one's taboos on others, listing nineteen such taboos. Some of them clearly deal with personal preferences such as "driving certain cars, wearing certain jewelry . . . getting a face lift, drinking coffee, eating certain foods."[53] Then he also lists "going to the movies or live theater, . . . not having a 'quiet time' every morning or at least every day, . . . wearing certain clothing, . . . listening to certain music,"[54] and others. The scriptural principles taught in Matthew 15:18-20, Philippians 4:8, and other places should surely be applied to these activities. Evil thinking produces sinful action. If adultery is wrong, how can watching it, reading or singing about it, and otherwise feeding the mind on it be right? Likewise, does not Scripture teach us modesty in both dress and conduct (I Tim. 2:9; 3:2)? Although one must beware of establishing human standards of spirituality, in the light of passages such as Psalm 1:1-3, Joshua 1:8, and Romans 12:2, one cannot stress enough the importance of a continual fellowship with God through prayer and Bible study such as is found in a daily "quiet time." Furthermore, a verse such as II Corinthians 4:16 (which speaks of the renewal "day by day" of "the inward man") surely indicates that a Christian's devotional life is to be no haphazard thing. Believers must let principles of the Word of God change them (II Cor. 3:18). Man has no right to impose his own will on Scripture.

This is not to imply that Swindoll favors adultery, immodesty in dress and conduct, or impure thinking. His life, ministry, testimony, and personal response to me in discussing this issue say otherwise in a "loud and clear" fashion. The point is that while Scripture has no clear statements about what cars we drive and whether we drink coffee, biblical principles do speak clearly to the content of what is portrayed in the movies or live theater, what is sung in music, and how Christians dress. These matters have a positive or negative moral content and are either consistent with or contrary to the holiness of God. Decisions that Christians make in these areas are not just personal taboos which we are not to impose on others. They are decisions which are made in obedience to or in violation of clear biblical principles. Swindoll has left that issue clouded.

Guidelines for Setting Standards

Fortunately some leaders have given thought to how they set standards for the ministries in which they are involved. Les Ollila, president of Northland Baptist Bible College, has arrived at several conclusions. He states that there are "individual standards and institutional standards."[55] Practically, parents with three or four children in a home can maintain godly standards with different rules than can a Christian college with hundreds in a dormitory.

In determining standards Ollila constructs a three-step model. It involves defining purpose, principle, and then policy.[56] The home, church, or ministry must first understand its purpose. Ultimately that purpose is to glorify God and to reflect His holiness. The home, church, or ministry will state its purpose in a way consistent with its own work. After defining its purpose, the organization will seek out principles. Those principles for the college where Ollila serves as president are "always biblical."[57] These principles apply to educational objectives, morality, social development, and so on. As the church, home, or institution applies those principles to its individual situation, the policy takes shape. These are the standards and rules by which people in a ministry or given setting live and work. An institution is able to arrive at policies, or standards, which reflect Bible principles because it begins with biblical purposes and principles. People who are involved in the ministries are able to understand the leadership and follow willingly because they see that there is a biblical foundation to the structure. Any Christian who has trouble living in such an environment will probably not be in harmony with God's Spirit and His Word in his personal life. A person who has developed a passion for God's holiness will likely be content in such a frame of reference.

Conclusion

The idea of separation is woven into the fabric of holiness. The truth of God's holiness affects the Christian's life and will result in an imitation of that holiness by the believer. God's holiness demanded actions reflecting His holiness in the life of the individual in the Old Testament economy. In the New Testament economy, the believer will desire to imitate God's holiness. Ephesians 4:17–5:18 and other passages show how holiness specifically affects the believer's life. Holiness is possible because of the work of Christ. Those who have received Him are positionally holy. As God uses His Word, the indwelling Spirit, and chastening, the Christian progressively imitates God's holiness. Holiness is also prospective and will be completed in the glorified believer in heaven.

Separation from sin is not isolation from the world. The purpose for the believer's holy position and practice is so that he can testify of God's saving power in the world. Personal separation from sin complements evangelism.

Conformity to a standard of conduct does not make one holy or spiritual. The believer is to desire to imitate God's holiness. That inner desire, motivated by love and empowered by the Holy Spirit who fills the surrendered believer, will produce outward victory over sin and conformity to the standards of God's holiness as they are outlined in the New Testament. The believer must apply Bible principles to activities about which the Scriptures do not specifically speak.

Notes

[1] William F. Arndt and F. Wilbur Gingrich, *A Greek-English Lexicon of the New Testament* (Chicago: University of Chicago Press, 1957), p. 524.

[2] I Cor. 11:1 New King James Version.

[3] Arndt and Gingrich, p. 803.

[4] Dana F. Kellerman, ed. *New Webster's Dictionary of the English Language* (New York: Delair Publishing Company, Inc., 1981), p. 1342.

[5] The verb used is the aorist imperative form of ἀναστρέφω (*anastrepho*) which means "to pass." Figuratively it is used "of human conduct—act, behave, conduct oneself, or live in the sense of the practice of certain principles." Arndt and Gingrich, p. 60.

[6] Kenneth S. Wuest, "First Peter," *Wuest's Word Studies from the Greek New Testament* (Grand Rapids: Eerdmans, 1980 reprint), 2:40.

[7] Charles R. Erdman, *The General Epistles* (Philadelphia, Westminster Press, 1919), p. 60.

[8] J.N.D. Kelly, *A Commentary on the Epistles of Peter and Jude* (Grand Rapids: Baker Book House, 1981 reprint), p. 71.

[9] C. D. Ginsburg, "Leviticus," *Ellicott's Commentary on the Whole Bible*, ed. Charles John Ellicott (Grand Rapids: Zondervan, 1954 edition), 1:421.

[10] The fear of God is biblically defined as a reverence for God because of His character and creative power (Ps. 33:4-9; 89:7), and a trust in God (Ps. 33:18). The element of terror is largely absent from this concept (Exod. 20:20). *The Scofield Reference Bible*, ed. C. I. Scofield (New York: Oxford University Press, 1945), p. 670, calls it "a phrase of Old Testament piety, meaning reverential trust with hatred of evil." A more complete analysis reveals four major evidences of the fear of God in the life of the believer, namely, (1) hatred of evil (Prov. 8:13; Job 1:1, 8; 2:3; Prov. 3:7; 16:6); (2) knowledge of holiness (Prov. 9:10); (3) service for God (Josh. 24:14; I Sam. 12:24); and (4) obedience to God's commandments (Eccles. 12:13). Some New Testament examples of its use are I Peter 2:17, where the idea of reverence is emphasized; Hebrews 12:28, where both reverence and service are stressed; Revelation 15:4, where reverence and God's holiness meet; and II Corinthians 7:1, where reverence, holiness, and hatred of sin converge.

[11] Arndt and Gingrich, p. 47.

[12] W. E. Vine, *Vine's Expository Dictionary of New Testament Words* (McLean: MacDonald Publishing Company, n.d.), p. 133.

[13] Arndt and Gingrich, p. 422.

[14] Ibid., p. 418.

[15] Arndt and Gingrich, p. 489, describe the word μαλακός (*malakos*) as "catamites, men and boys who allow themselves to be misused homosexually."

[16]The word used here is ἀρσενοκοίτης (*arsenokoitēs*), which Arndt and Gingrinch, p. 109, define as "a male homosexual."

[17]The word λοίδορος (*loidoros*), according to Vine, p. 294, signifies "abusive, railing, reviling."

[18]Arndt and Gingrich, p. 108, state that this word, ἅρπαξ (*harpax*), is translated "robber," and may be "perhaps better swindler."

[19]There is some debate among scholars concerning the phrase "in spirit." Some hold that it refers to the spirit of man rather than to the third person of the Trinity. F. F. Bruce, *The Epistle to the Ephesians* (Old Tappan: Fleming H. Revell Company, 1974 reprint), p. 110, points out that the identical phrase is used in Ephesians 2:22, 3:5, and 6:18 and that each use has the work of the Holy Spirit in view. This is compelling reason to conclude that the phrase refers to the Holy Spirit here also.

[20]H.C.G. Moule, *Ephesian Studies* (London: Pickering and Inglis Ltd., n.d.), p. 267.

[21]Lewis Sperry Chafer, *Systematic Theology* (Dallas: Dallas Seminary Press, 1948), 7:274-84, points out that the Father (I Thess. 5:23) and the Son (Heb. 2:11; 10:10) also sanctify. Their work of sanctification appears to relate more to the believer's position as sanctified than to the ongoing progression of sanctification where the Spirit, the Word, and discipline are the means of sanctification.

[22]Charles Hodge, *Systematic Theology* (Grand Rapids: Eerdmans, 1977 reprint), 3:221.

[23]A. Skevington Wood, "Ephesians" in *The Expositor's Bible Commentary*, ed. Frank E. Gaebelein (Grand Rapids: Zondervan, 1978), 11:63.

[24]John Eadie, *Commentary on the Epistle to the Ephesians* (Grand Rapids: Zondervan, 1979 reprint), p. 340.

[25]"unbridled lust," Thayer, p. 79.

[26]"the iniquity of lustful, luxurious, profligate living," ibid., p. 21.

[27]"indignation which has arisen gradually and become more settled." ibid., p. 293.

[28]"anger . . . boiling up and soon subsiding again," ibid., p. 293.

[29]A. T. Robertson, *Word Pictures in the New Testament* (Grand Rapids: Baker Book House, 1931), 4:541, speaks of speech which is "rotten, putrid, like fruit."

[30]"outcry," ibid., p. 541.

[31]"blasphemy," Thayer, pp. 102-3.

[32]"ill will, desire to injure," ibid., p. 320.

[33]Thayer, pp. 531-32, gives his first definition as "illicit sexual intercourse in general." The word is generally accepted as being the generic New Testament term for immorality.

[34]"base, or dishonorable," ibid., p. 17.

[35]Thayer, p. 263, states that in the evil sense the word is used for "scurrility, ribaldry, low jesting."

[36]William Hendricksen, *Exposition of Ephesians,* New Testament Commentary (Grand Rapids: Baker Book House, 1979 reprint), p. 218.

[37]*Light* is to be understood as a synonym for God's holiness (I John 1:5).

[38]Homer A. Kent, "Philippians" in *The Expositor's Bible Commentary,* ed. Frank E. Gaebelein (Grand Rapids: Zondervan, 1978), 11:152.

[39]Eadie, pp. 21-22.

[40]Kurt DeHaan, *I'm Not a Legalist, Am I?* (Grand Rapids: Radio Bible Class, 1988), p. 3.

[41]The part of legalism that deals with conformity to the law for salvation is a critical area worthy of discussion. The idea of salvation by works of some kind is an ever-present heresy. It is, however, outside the focus of this study. Suffice it to say that the passages such as Romans 3:21-28; Galatians 2:16; and Ephesians 2:8-9 clearly demonstrate the Bible's teaching that salvation is by faith in Christ and wholly apart from any human effort.

[42]Douglas R. McLachlan, "Charting a Straight Course (II)—Legalism," *The Central Testimony,* Winter 1987, p. 1.

[43]DeHaan, p. 3.

[44]McLachlan, p. 2.

[45]Charles R. Swindoll, *The Grace Awakening* (Dallas: Word Publishing, 1990), p. 81.

[46]Ken R. Pulliam, "Christian Standards Are Not Legalism," *Frontline,* September/October, 1991, p. 7.

[47]DeHaan, p. 22.

[48]Swindoll, p. 132.

[49]Pulliam, p. 7.

[50]Merrill F. Unger, *The New Unger's Bible Dictionary,* ed. R. K. Harrison (Chicago: Moody Press, 1988 ed.), p. 999.

[51]Vine, p. 112.

[52]Ibid., p. 174.

[53]Swindoll, pp. 159-60.

[54]Ibid., p. 159.

[55]Les Ollila, interview by author, Dunbar, Wisconsin, 22 November, 1991.

[56]Ibid.

[57]Ibid.

3

ECCLESIASTICAL SEPARATION

When Harold John Ockenga introduced New Evangelicalism, he repudiated the strategy of separation. It should be apparent at this point, then, that Ockenga repudiated a strategy that is firmly rooted in the holiness of God. That repudiation of separatism also had a negative impact on another biblically commanded strategy, namely evangelism. Ockenga, in fact, rejected the strategy of separatism as it applies to virtually every area of the ministry. He announced that New Evangelicalism would be promoted through several means. Its "organizational front" included the National Association of Evangelicals, the World Evangelical Fellowship, apologetic literature, Fuller Theological Seminary and other seminaries, *Christianity Today* as the movement's printed voice, and Billy Graham as its spokesman.[1] In naming Billy Graham as New Evangelicalism's mouthpiece,[2] Ockenga specifically rejected separatism as it applies to evangelism.

A few months before Ockenga made his announcement, *Christian Life* magazine articulated this same philosophy when it observed, "The fundamentalist watchword is 'Ye should earnestly contend for the faith.' The evangelical emphasis is 'Ye must be born again.' "[3] That statement denigrated separation in order to emphasize evangelism. Yet this statement, which seems to set evangelism and separation at odds with each other, cannot be supported from Scripture. In fact the opposite is true. Scripture ties evangelism and separation together as companions. The best-known New Testament passage which deals with separation also deals with evangelism.

In II Corinthians 5 Paul explains the power of the gospel to change men's lives (v. 17). He then declares that God had given him a ministry of reconciling men to God (vv. 18-19), and as an "ambassador for Christ," he pleads with men to be reconciled to God (v. 20). He then opens the next section by saying, "We then, as workers together with him, beseech you also that ye receive not the grace of God in vain. (For he saith, I have heard thee in a time accepted, and in the day of salvation have I succoured thee: behold, now is the accepted time; behold, now is the day of salvation)" (II Cor. 6:1-2). The aim of this entire section of II Corinthians seems to be expressed in Paul's desire to give "no offence in anything" (v. 3), "but in all things approving ourselves as the ministers of God" (v. 4). Paul desired to "commend,"[4] or "approve," himself and the ministry as above reproach.

Paul's fervent plea for men to be saved sprang from that desire. Further examination of the passage shows he also sought to commend himself and the ministry by his endurance in all the circumstances and trials he faced (vv. 4-10). He sought to commend the ministry with his tender heart and affection for the Corinthians (vv. 11-13). The last way in which Paul sought to commend himself and the ministry was by consistent separation (6:14–7:1). This foundational passage begins with evangelism and closes with separation. It is obvious that Ockenga's repudiation of separatism will not stand up in the face of careful scrutiny according to scriptural standards. The forced division between the strategies of evangelism and separatism is an unnatural dichotomy when evaluated by biblical standards. It is also clear that ecclesiastical separation—the separation of the local church from unbelief—flows from the holiness of God. The practice of separation has as its goal "perfecting holiness in the fear of God" (II Cor. 7:1).

This study has demonstrated so far that separation is part of the concept of holiness, and that personal separation derives from the idea of holiness. The purpose of this chapter is to demonstrate that ecclesiastical separation also flows from the idea of holiness. The New Testament teaches that the local church[5] is to separate itself from all theological unbelief and from the false teachers who promote it.

Old Testament Background

The Old Testament contains a wealth of information on the subject of separation. This study could never exhaust all of that information, nor is that its purpose.[6] There are some Old Testament passages, however, which need to be considered as background for this chapter.

Separation from Idolatry

God's holiness demanded that Israel separate itself from all idolatrous religions. God warned that the worship of Molech would "profane my holy name" (Lev. 20:3). He warned against spiritism and then commanded worship and service because of His holiness (Lev. 20:7-8). In Leviticus 21:1-8 God set standards for the priests who ministered in the tabernacle. The priests had to be pure ceremonially (vv. 1-4), pure from idolatrous practice (v. 5), and pure morally (vv. 7-8). The reason for this purity is God's holiness (vv. 6-8). Because God is holy, He commands His people to renounce all false religion.

Separation Between Clean and Unclean

God speaks through Ezekiel and charges the priests in Israel with "profan[ing] my holy things" (Ezek. 22:26). The priests had "put no difference between the holy and the profane, neither have they shewed difference between the unclean and the clean." Plumtre and Whitelaw explain the nature of the offence which God rebuked: "Their guilt was that they blurred over the distinction . . . in what we have learned to call . . . the ceremonial ordinances of the Law, and so blunted their keenness of perception in regard to analogous moral distinctions."[7] Prophetically, Ezekiel looks forward to the day when the priests will again teach those distinctions to God's people.

Influence on New Testament Teaching

The Old Testament teaching about separation from false gods and about the difference between the holy and profane undergirds the New Testament teaching on separation. The foremost New Testament passage and the one which will be examined in detail is II Corinthians 6:14–7:1. The plea "Wherefore come out from among them, and be ye separate, and touch not the unclean thing" (II Cor. 6:17) is a quotation from Isaiah. Just before the prophecy of Christ's death and glorification (Isa. 52:13–53:12), God speaks to the captive nation and to the priests in Egypt (Isa. 52:4) and commands, "Depart ye, depart ye, go ye out from thence, touch no unclean thing; go ye out of the midst of her; be ye clean, that bear the vessels of the Lord" (Isa. 52:11).[8]

Paul's condemnation of idolatry makes it clear that the Old Testament teaching on separation from idolatry, based on the holiness of God, is also part of the foundation of the New Testament revelation.

II Corinthians 6:14–7:1

This is the keystone passage in the New Testament which deals with separation. It brings forward the Old Testament principles into the New Testament, and it also relates the matter of separation to the doctrine of God's holiness. Paul says:

> Be ye not unequally yoked together with unbelievers: for what fellowship hath righteousness with unrighteousness? and what communion hath light with darkness? And what concord hath Christ with Belial? or what part hath he that believeth with an infidel? And what agreement hath the temple of God with idols? for ye are the temple of the living God; as God hath said, I will dwell in them, and walk in them; and I will be their God, and they shall be my people. Wherefore come out from among them, and be ye separate, saith the Lord, and touch not the unclean thing; and I will receive you, and I will be a Father unto you, and ye shall be my sons and daughters, saith the Lord Almighty. Having therefore these promises, dearly beloved, let us cleanse ourselves from all filthiness of the flesh and spirit, perfecting holiness in the fear of God (II Cor. 6:14–7:1).

The Absolute of Separation

The command to separate is unequivocal. It cannot be explained away, limited, or ignored. Believers are simply commanded to stop the practice of an unequal yoke with unbelievers. This statement sets the parameters for the discussion.

There are those who have attempted to state that separatists misapply this passage when they apply it to separation from unbelief today. Donald Grey Barnhouse was representative of this position:

> "Oh," says someone, "but God says, 'Come out from among them and be ye separate!' " Well, now I'm just not going to let you get away with applying that verse to any phase of the church. If you're honest with the epistle to the Corinthians, "Come out

from among them" was to come out from the temple of Venus and temple of Jupiter, where they poured out libations to the demon gods, and where one temple in Corinth owned more than 10,000 prostitutes and sodomites that were sold by the hour to the thousands of sailors and workmen that transhipped the goods of the ancient world across the narrow Isthmus of Corinth. "Come out from among *them*, and be separate."[9]

It should be noted that the commentators universally disregard this attempt to limit the passage, and they acknowledge that the principles of the passage apply directly to unbelief.[10]

Meaning of the Yoke

The term "unequally yoked" (v. 14) describes a working relationship. The Old Testament prohibits the crossbreeding (Lev. 19:19) and yoking (Deut. 22:10) of diverse kinds of animals.[11] Wiersbe points out that the ox was a clean animal and the ass was unclean. He goes on to say, "Furthermore, they have two opposite natures and would not even work well together. It would be cruel to bind them to each other. In the same way it is wrong for believers to be yoked together with unbelievers."[12]

The emphasis is that the local church is not to place itself in a working relationship with unbelievers. It is wrong for the local church to affiliate with an association, convention, council of churches, or any service agency, where it is working with unbelievers in an attempt to do God's work. To cooperate with unbelievers in an evangelistic crusade is equally wrong. To work with unbelievers in a missionary enterprise at home or on an overseas field is also wrong. Alford demonstrates the general application of this principle: "The following exhortations are general, and hardly to be pressed as applying only to partaking of meats offered to idols . . . or to marriage with unbelievers . . . but regard all possible connexion and participation—all leanings toward a returning to heathenism which might be bred by too great familiarity with heathens."[13]

It should be noted again that this passage begins with evangelism and closes with separation. To be effective in winning the lost to Christ, a local church must separate itself from unbelievers. The distinction between Christ and unbelievers must stand out in bold relief. That distinction lends power to the gospel and the work of evangelism. The gospel saves men from sin and its corruption, and the agencies and people who minister the gospel must demonstrate the saving power of the gospel by separation from those who deny it. To cooperate with unbelievers is to blur the line that God has drawn.

Douglas Groothuis understands this principle, for example, as it applies to the current New Age Movement. His point is that the New Age movement is occultic, demonic, and therefore diametrically opposed to the gospel message. He says of the New Age movement: "There is absolutely no way to Christianize it."[14] After briefly reviewing the Bible's teaching on separation from the occult and from all sin, he states, "The separation theme is crucial for confronting the New Age."[15] He goes on to make very clear the fact that the believer is to have nothing to do with New Age practices or lifestyle. His article is clear in stating that separation from evil is the means to the end of declaring the gospel message to those who are caught up in it. His conclusion about separation demands attention: "If Christians hope to confront error effectively, we cannot let ourselves become prisoners of what we are confronting. We must be separate."[16]

Separation Not Isolation

The command to separation is not a command to isolation. This was seen in Chapter Two, which dealt with the personal separation of the believer from unholiness in his lifestyle. This important truth relates to ecclesiastical separation as well. The local church is not to yoke up with unbelievers and work with them in spiritual endeavors. Yet neither the church nor the believer can isolate himself from contact with unbelievers. To isolate oneself from contact with unbelievers would be to leave the world (I Cor. 5:9-10). God's intent is exactly the opposite. The believer and the local church are to be in the world, separated from sin and unbelievers in lifestyle and cooperative effort, in order to proclaim clearly and forcefully the gospel's power to save men from sin. Separation is a strategy which is to be employed in tandem with evangelism; it is the complement of evangelism.

Separation Complete

The command to separation is complete. Lenski is eloquent in his statement that God's people must separate from any shade of unbelief: " 'With unbelievers' mentions the extreme. Some read this . . . as if this forbids only the extreme. . . . This is true with regard to total unbelief which makes open mock of Christ. It includes every bit of unbelief, every repudiation of Christ's doctrine, every little yoke that is not of the true faith. Besser is right when in these yokes he finds a reference to unionism with those who repudiate any part of the Word."[17]

The Analogies of Separation

Paul follows his command to separate with reasons for the command. He asks five rhetorical questions. There are two outstanding characteristics of his questions: incompatible realms and incongruous relationships.

Incompatible Realms

In each of his questions (II Cor. 6:14-16) Paul sets the believer in stark contrast to the unbeliever. Lenski describes how Paul contrasts the "inner quality" of believers and unbelievers ("righteousness" and "unrighteousness"), the "powers which produce them" ("light" and "darkness"), the "personal rulers" of the two realms ("Christ" and "Belial"), the "personal subjects," ("he that believeth" and "an infidel"),[18] and "the persons in their ultimate relation" ("the temple of God" and "idols").[19] To reinforce the fact that "ye are the temple of the living God" (II Cor. 6:16), Paul again quotes from the Old Testament, this time from Leviticus 26:11 and Ezekiel 37:27.[20] These questions combine to form a strong reminder that the realms of faith and of unbelief are utterly incompatible.

Incongruous Relationships

Paul also uses five words to describe the relationship which would exist between believers and unbelievers were they to be unequally yoked. He states that between these two contrasting parties there can be no fellowship; no communion, or "sharing";[21] no concord, or "symphony";[22] no part, or "portion";[23] and no agreement, or "putting together the votes" (a legislative image describing the joining of several factions into a coalition to fashion a majority).[24]

When the nature of the believer is contrasted with that of the unbeliever, it is incongruous that there should be any fellowship, sharing, harmony, part, or forming of a coalition with them. One imagines that Paul vividly remembered his commission on the Damascus road where Jesus sent him "to open their eyes, and to turn them from darkness to light, and from the power of Satan unto God" (Acts 26:18). He would cringe at the thought that he could be yoked with unbelievers in the work of turning men "from darkness to light, and from the power of Satan unto God." Nothing could be more illogical or unreasonable.

The Admonition to Separation

"Scripture is reinforced by Scripture."[25] Paul reinforces his Old Testament citation about their relationship to God (II Cor. 6:16) by citing the Isaiah 52:11 passage when he commands them to "come out from among them, and be ye separate, saith the Lord, and touch not the unclean thing" (II Cor. 6:17). The local church is to "come out" from alliances which yoke it to the forces of unbelief and denial of the Word of God. This command is unmistakable and could not be clearer. The church is to be clean and pure from unbelief and the kingdom of darkness (II Cor. 6:14; Col. 1:13) as it seeks to bring men to Christ.

The Affirmations of Separation

This passage indicates an intimate relationship between God and His people. God dwells among His people (II Cor. 6:16). After He commands separation, God makes some promises to His people. These promises to be a Father to His people and that they will be His children are again Old Testament quotations, perhaps from II Samuel 7:14, but more likely from Isaiah 43:6 and Ezekiel 20:34.[26] The promise that God's people will be His sons and daughters "connotes all the high rights of sonship, and 'daughters' does the same."[27] For the Christian, the way to intimate fellowship and full blessing from the Lord is the way of separation from sin and unbelief.

The Applications of Separation

Paul exhorts God's people to claim God's promises and to perform two actions. The first exhortation is to "cleanse ourselves from all filthiness of the flesh and spirit" (II Cor. 7:1). This cleansing is apparently a progressive work in the believer's life.[28] Both the flesh and spirit are to be cleansed. That which defiles the flesh (Eph. 4:25-29) and that which defiles the spirit (Eph. 4:31) must be put away. As the believer is to cleanse himself, so the local church is to cleanse itself. This exhortation applied by the local church would apply to the unequal yoke with unbelievers in work and fellowship, and from carnal, fleshly methods as well. It speaks of cleansing from "all sorts of filthiness, physical, moral, mental, ceremonial."[29]

The second exhortation which applies separation is that the believer and the local church are to be "perfecting holiness in the fear of God" (II Cor. 7:1). This perfection of holiness is to be "aggressive and progressive."[30] The present participle form of ἐπιτελέω (epiteleō) indicates an ongoing effort to "complete, accomplish"[31] holiness in the fear of God. Purity and separation in God's eyes are not merely the absence of evil. To be sure, the church and the believer must cleanse themselves from sin. Positively, the believer and the church are to seek and to be perfected by holiness.

Summation

Ecclesiastical separation (earlier defined as the separation of the local church from unbelief) is rooted firmly in the holiness of God, as is the biblical teaching on personal separation. Separation is an integral part of the Christian ministry. The great goal is to win men to Christ in this day of salvation. To that end, the minister and the local church must demonstrate the integrity of the ministry before men. Purity in life and the practice of the ministry validates the message that delivers men from sin and hell. Ministries must be separated from all personal or corporate moral uncleanness, and they must complete holiness in the fear of God.

Other New Testament Scriptures

The New Testament contains a profusion of passages that deal with the subject of separation from false teachers and false doctrine.

Warnings Against False Teachers

Jesus' Warnings

Jesus warns His disciples of the dangers of false prophets on at least two occasions. His words in Matthew 7 are particularly important: "Beware of false prophets, which come to you in sheep's clothing, but inwardly they are ravening wolves. Ye shall know them by their fruits. Do men gather grapes of thorns, or figs of thistles?" (Matt. 7:15-16). The first fact of note in Christ's statement is His use of the figure of wolves. False prophets appear in sheep's clothing, masquerading as God's children (John 10:1-16; Acts 20:28; I Pet. 5:1-4); but they are wolves, or enemies of the sheep. Paul uses this same figure of speech to warn the church at Ephesus of the deceptive nature of these false teachers (Acts 20:29). They are "Christ-merchants,"[32] who are covetous. Referring to what may be considered the ultimate deception, Jesus also warns of false teachers who will appear claiming to be Christ Himself (Matt. 24:4-5). He cautions His followers not to be deceived by them.

The second important fact in Jesus' warning concerns the marks of the false prophets. He warns His followers that false prophets will be known by their fruits (Matt. 7:16-20). It hardly seems coincidental that so many later passages in the New Testament expose the moral character of false teachers along with their false teaching (Phil. 3:18-19; II Pet. 2:10-22; Jude 8, 16).

Paul's Warnings

Paul's writings are replete with warnings about false teachers. In his farewell sermon to the elders of the Ephesian church he warns of "grievous wolves" who apparently are false teachers from outside the church (Acts 20:29). He cautions the Roman church concerning those "which cause divisions and offenses contrary to the doctrine which ye have learned" (Rom. 16:17). The standard by which they are to be judged is doctrine, and Paul's instruction to the church is to "mark them . . . and avoid them."

Paul warns the Corinthian church against false teachers in at least two passages. He states that these teachers "corrupt the word of God" (II Cor. 2:17). The verb *corrupt* means to "trade in, peddle, huckster."[33] Paul distances himself from such false teachers in II Corinthians 4:2, where he denies "handl[ing] the word of God deceitfully," that is, he does not "falsify" or "adulterate"[34] the Word of God.

In II Corinthians 11 the apostle deals in some detail with false teachers. He again stresses their deceptive nature (v. 3) and states that their doctrine presents a false Christ, another spirit, and a false gospel (v. 4). Paul calls them deceivers (v. 13; "deceitful workers" in the KJV), using the same word for deceit that he uses in II Corinthians 4:2. These are the falsifiers and adulterators of Scripture. He goes on to call them "false apostles . . . transforming themselves into the apostles of Christ" (v. 13). They are Satan's ministers who use his methods (v. 14-15).

Paul warns the Galatian churches about false teachers as well. This is the first book in which he attacks the Judaizers, those who want to add the works of the law to the gospel. He identifies their gospel as a false gospel (Gal. 1:6-7) and pronounces the teachers of a false gospel "accursed" (Gal. 1:8-9).

Paul also alerts the Philippian church to the dangers of false teachers. He tells them to "beware of dogs, beware of evil workers, beware of the concision" (Phil. 3:2). These are the Judaizers who add the works of the law to the gospel. The word *concision* means a "mutilation, cutting in pieces."[35] It appears to be a play on words, describing those "who insist on worthless mutilation of the flesh, and something which denies the all-sufficiency of Christ."[36] Paul may be further alluding to the fact that "circumcision results in (spiritual) destruction."[37] He contrasts their doctrine with his own faith in Christ and His righteousness (3:9). He later calls them "enemies of the cross of Christ" (3:18) and describes their moral character (3:19).

Paul also warns Titus about false teachers, in this case, the Judaizers (Titus 1:10-14). In Titus 3:10-11 he warns him about the heretic, or the man who is "factious, causing divisions."[38] After two admonitions this man is to be rejected, that is, the church is to "beg off from" him.[39]

Peter's Warnings

In II Peter 2, the Apostle Peter devotes an entire chapter to exposing false teachers. Peter dedicates the major portion of the passage (vv. 3-22) to the moral character of the false teachers. He touches on their doctrinal deviation by stating that they "shall bring in damnable heresies, even denying the Lord that bought them" (v. 1). These false teachers display a rebellious attitude toward the authority of Christ. The word translated "lord" is δεσπότης (*despotēs*). The word is "the correlative of slave, δοῦλος [*doulos*], and hence denoted absolute ownership and uncontrolled power."[40]

With His blood Christ purchased those who know Him (Eph. 1:7). He is Master and Lord of His children. The false teacher rebels at that authority. In II Peter 3:1-4 Peter also warns against those who deny the doctrine of the Lord's return.

John's Warnings

John includes several strong warnings against false teachers in his epistles (I John 2:21-26; 4:1-3; II John 7-11). As Peter seems to center on the character of false teachers, John makes the doctrine of Christ the standard by which the false teachers are judged. Christ's messiahship (I John 2:22) and His incarnation (I John 4:2; II John 7) are the litmus tests that prove or disprove the veracity of the teacher.

Jude's Warnings

The entire Epistle of Jude is a caution against false teachers. As far as Jude is concerned, "the faith" (v. 3)—or the whole system of revealed truth which is the "body of faith or belief, doctrine"[41]—is in jeopardy. The false teachers distort the doctrine of grace and deny the same authority of Christ (v. 4) of which Peter spoke. Jude also speaks extensively (vv. 8-16) of the depraved character of the false teachers.

Warnings Against False Doctrine

All the writers of Scripture who warn of false teachers also deal with false doctrine. The inspired authors declare that the gospel, the doctrine of Christ, the Lord's return, and the whole body of revealed truth are under attack. Beyond these statements Paul warns Timothy several times of false doctrine.

Warnings to Timothy

In his first epistle to Timothy, the Apostle Paul gives several warnings concerning false teaching. He cautions Timothy against "fables and endless genealogies" (I Tim. 1:3-6), apparently referring to speculations by the Gnostics about spirits.[42] Paul further offers examples of those shipwrecked in their faith because of this false teaching (vv. 18-20). Paul admonishes Timothy about those who will depart from the Faith in the last days (I Tim. 4:1-3). These men, says the apostle, will succumb to apostasy, "a standing away from their original position."[43] Paul condemns their doctrine as "demon's teaching"[44] (v. 1; "doctrines of devils" in KJV), false doctrine propounded by devils. The apostle warns Timothy of those who do not consent, or "attach themselves,"[45] to wholesome words. Guthrie observes that this statement probably refers to teaching about Christ or revealed truth about Him.[46]

Paul issues a strong warning against false doctrine in II Timothy 2:16-23. He begins by reiterating to Timothy the need to shun "profane and vain babblings" (v. 16). He is referring to what Hendricksen calls "unholy, useless disputes about fictitious genea- logical histories and hair splitting debates about niceties in the law of Moses."[47] He uses the pejorative term to describe the nature of the teaching and describes its fruit as "more ungodliness" (v. 16). He identifies two major proponents of this false doctrine as Hymenaeus and Philetus (v. 17) and names the false doctrine these men taught as a wrong view of the resurrection (v. 18). Fairbairn demonstrates that the denial of the resurrection would be common to all false sects in the Greek culture since the doctrine was foreign to Greek thinking.[48] This was an "incipient gnosticism."[49]

The commands to separate from this false doctrine are clear. Timothy is told to "shun" this doctrine (v. 16). The command is given to "depart from iniquity" (v. 19), and the blessing of God is promised to the man who will "purge himself from these" (v. 21). The context of the passage clearly indicates that the iniquity from which one is to depart is the erroneous doctrine which Paul exposed. Unquestionably, "Paul is admonishing Timothy to separate himself from false teachers."[50]

Holiness and Separation from False Doctrine

It must be noted that the concept of holiness relates to the issue of separation from wrong doctrine. Timothy, and those today who obey Paul's command to separate from error, are "sanctified, and meet for the master's use, and prepared unto every good work" (II Tim. 2:21). He will be "set apart to noble and holy uses."[51] False doctrine has one effect, namely "increas[ing] unto more ungodli- ness" (v. 16), and it is "iniquity" (v. 19). The teaching is that the doctrine against which Paul warns is not simply wrong but com- pletely sinful and unholy. The preacher, to be clean and usable in his ministry must "purge himself from these" (v. 21).

Analysis of the New Evangelical Position on Separation

It is important to analyze the position on separation which those who embrace the New Evangelical philosophy hold.

Ockenga's Position

Harold Ockenga made his position clear in a commentary he authored on II Thessalonians. In commenting on Chapter 3, he writes on "The Church's Doctrine of Separation." He makes four major points.

Statement of Ockenga's Position

Ockenga's first premise is that churches are to separate from those who are disorderly, but believers are not to separate from apostate churches. He states,

> It is very careless exegesis to use this text to justify individual Christians' withdrawal from Christian churches as apostate when there are some members who are not maintaining consistency of testimony either in belief or action. It is the church that is to exercise the discipline and to withdraw itself from the disorderly. There is an interesting analogy between this passage of Scripture and II Corinthians 6:17, 18. The Corinthian Christians were not told to come out from the church but as a church they were told to separate themselves from those people who practiced idolatry and were still in unbelief.[52]

Ockenga's second premise is that apostasy does justify separation when the "parent body"[53] has forsaken its scriptural moorings. His third premise is that there is a form of unbelief which may be permitted to exist within the churches. This is where he reveals his nonseparatist philosophy of staying in those churches. He says,

> Some believers have earnestly tried to purify their congregations and denominations but have failed in the attempt. Therefore, they have separated themselves from the organization, believing that they were acting on Biblical authority. This has been the cause of many divisions within the church. Some go to the extreme of cutting off from fellowship all of those who are not sincerely convinced of the unbelief in the churches of which they are members. Thus, even Bible-believing Christians have been divided into two groups with the resulting confusion,

misunderstanding and weakness. Effort which ought to go toward the advancement of missions, evangelism and Christian education is now used to condemn and criticize fellow Christians who sincerely work within their churches.[54]

This extended quotation demonstrates that Ockenga decries the separation from apostasy that he had just previously said was the churches' right to exercise. Ockenga's last premise is that in II Timothy 2:16-21 Paul advocates that instead of separating from men who had erred from the truth that Christians "seek to recover these men from their error by instructing them in meekness."[55]

Evaluation

Ockenga's argument ignores the real issue. What is a believer to do when he finds himself in an apostate church or denomination? Certainly the Christian must make an honest effort to rectify the situation. John Ashbrook states as two of his axioms that "Scripture commands us to reprove apostasy" and that "Scripture teaches us that we must purge unbelief if we can."[56] If the believer cannot correct the situation, he has no choice but to separate himself from the apostate organization. If breaking the unequal yoke constitutes obedience to God for the local church, it surely must also constitute obedience for the individual believer who leaves an apostate local church.

Ockenga's interpretation of II Timothy 2:16-21 is difficult to understand. Although Paul counseled Timothy to seek the recovery of Hymenaeus and Philetus, he also exposed their error. His plain command was "Let every one that nameth the name of Christ depart from iniquity" (II Tim. 2:19). In II Timothy 2:22-24 Paul tells Timothy to "flee . . . youthful lusts" (v. 22), and to "avoid" false doctrine (v. 23). The exhortation to meek and patient instruction has as its aim the repentance of those who have erred (vv. 24-26). That exhortation in no way modifies the repeated commands to separate from unholy false doctrine.

Current Perspectives

It is important to understand a current assessment of the status of New Evangelicalism. Two recognized leaders of the New Evangelical (or simply evangelical, as they would call it) movement have commented on its current state. Kenneth S. Kantzer and Carl F. H. Henry have been involved in the movement from the beginning.

They have discussed a range of issues too wide for this study to evaluate completely, but some of their observations relate directly to this work.

Understanding Evangelicalism

After reviewing the history of the term *evangelical* from the time of Martin Luther, Kantzer gives a lucid definition of the term: "There is a group that have held to those basic, distinctive things with respect to the gospel; faith in Christ and our relationship to God through Him, *and* the authority of Scripture as the way by which we determine theology."[57]

Both Kantzer and Henry refer to the five fundamentals and other orthodox doctrines as distinctive of evangelicalism. Henry noted that two of the driving forces behind the National Association of Evangelicals at its founding in 1942 were that (1) "it had a doctrinal statement" (in contrast to the Federal Council of Churches) and (2) it sought to "overcome the hostility of the ecumenical bureaucracy" which had kept evangelicals out of the secular media.[58] Kantzer allows that his definition of evangelicalism leaves room for charismatics and others with whom he has profound theological disagreements. Henry states that from the beginning the NAE was a broad fellowship, including Pentecostals.[59]

Homogeneous Philosophy

The philosophical approach of New Evangelicalism remains virtually unchanged from 1957 to the present. Kantzer discusses the differences between fundamentalism and evangelicalism. He states that the difference is in "the strategic way to place Evangelical or Fundamentalist efforts,"[60] that is, the difference is whether their efforts are expended in a separatist or a nonseparatist frame of reference. He explains that fundamentalists believe that "separation from liberalism"[61] is necessary while Billy Graham has adopted the strategy of inviting modernists to cooperate in his evangelistic endeavors. He notes that this difference became a "practical cleavage as to strategy"[62] between the two groups.

What Kantzer recites is precisely the philosophy which Ockenga declared. In fact, Kantzer even repeatedly uses the word *strategy* that Ockenga used in his press release.[63] Henry further notes that "by appealing to evangelical remnants in the ecumeni- cally associated denominations Graham carried Fundamentalist evangelism into the very ecumenical movement whose leaders deplored it."[64] Kantzer evaluates the difference between funda- mentalism and evangelicalism by saying that "Fundamentalism is a part of Evangelicalism—that part that tends to be more separatis- tic than the other part."[65]

Failed Strategy

In the program from which these quotations come, moderator D. A. Carson asked Henry to evaluate the current status of the mainline denominations in America. Henry's response was that they are "no longer culturally definitive."[66] Carson suggested the word "irrele- vant,"[67] and Henry responded: "They are irrelevant."[68] Henry's statement is tantamount to admitting that the strategy of infiltration has failed. Patient attempts to persuade the apostate leaders instead of separating from them has failed. The evangelistic ministry of Billy Graham and others like him has also failed to reclaim the ecumenical denominations. Those who adopted the strategy of infiltrating those mainline, ecumenical denominations now say that they have not been reclaimed, but instead are of no consequence.

Conclusion

Summary

As the biblical teaching is examined it becomes apparent that the New Testament doctrine of separation is built on the foundation of Old Testament teaching. God taught His people that idolatry was a violation of His holiness, and He commanded His people to renounce false religion. The same principle, applied in the New Testament, demands that the local church abstain from work in cooperative association with unbelievers. It is apparent that the Bible's teaching on separation is a cohesive unit. The nature of God is always the same, and God's view of separation is consistently uniform between the Old Testament and the New Testament. The extensive use of the Old Testament in II Corinthians 6 indicates this fact.

Separation and evangelism cannot be divorced. The local church is to be separate from identification with unbelievers in order to effectively win unbelievers to faith in Christ. This study must state again a vital truth which has been noted several times previously. Separation is not isolation, but rather is the complement of evangelism.

Separation is necessary because the realms of God and Satan, and thus of the believer and the unbeliever, are complete opposites. They are as different as righteousness and lawlessness, and as light and darkness.

The purpose of separation is the ongoing effort by the local church or the believer to imitate the holiness of God. The holiness of God is the church's model to imitate in separating from unbelievers (II Cor. 7:1) and in separation from false doctrine (II Tim. 2:21). Scripture plainly teaches that God's holiness is the foundation of separation and that ecclesiastical separation, as well as personal separation, flows from that holiness.

Scripture warns against the lifestyle of false teachers. False doctrine leads to ungodliness and the fruit of the false teachers is their conduct, which is an insult to the holiness of God.

Practical Applications

Certain practical applications demand notice as this chapter concludes. This study of the biblical evidence directly affects the ministry.

Evangelism

Evangelism and separation are permanently wedded in Scripture and cannot be divorced. The major New Testament passage dealing with ecclesiastical separation begins with an impassioned evangelistic plea and concludes with a militant separatistic exhortation. Separation complements evangelism.

Scripture teaches that believers are to be "speaking the truth in love" (Eph. 4:15). Objectivity and kindness are both needed. In that spirit one must conclude that the New Evangelical division between evangelism and separatism is an unbiblical dichotomy. To forsake separatism in an attempt to emphasize evangelism produces two negative results. First, it completely ignores the clear biblical teaching about separation. Second, it distorts, weakens, and compromises the gospel message in evangelism.

The distortion of evangelism is sadly demonstrated in the ministry of Billy Graham, who, as noted, became the spokesman for New Evangelicalism. His work, which has included believers and unbelievers for years, has led to tragic compromises. This study will not document that long record of ecumenical, inclusive evangelism. William Ashbrook[69] and Ernest Pickering[70] have documented in detail the results of an evangelistic ministry which yokes believers with unbelievers. Those who espouse the philosophy of New Evangelicalism must confront the scriptural teaching that evangelism and separation are twin strategies which cannot be cut apart.

Biblical separatists cannot escape this study without also soberly reassessing their ministries in the light of the Scripture's teaching. All too often the separatist tends to emphasize his separatism and neglect evangelism. The biblical separatist needs to be reminded that *separation is not an end in itself*, but a biblical strategy to be employed in tandem with evangelism. To emphasize separation to the neglect of evangelism is to deaden the ministry and to distort both the purpose and the effect of separatism. Scripture teaches separation! The believer must imitate God's holiness and separate himself from sin. The local church must separate itself from unbelief in all forms. But the separated believer is to be a soulwinner (John 17:17, 20), and the separated local church is to be fervently evangelistic (II Cor. 6:1-2; 6:14–7:1). Every pastor is to "do the work of an evangelist" (II Tim. 4:5) as well as to "fight the good fight of faith" against false teaching (I Tim. 6:12).

Separatism

Those who have rejected separatism as a strategy face a dilemma. Kantzer refers to "the authority of Scripture as the way by which we determine theology."[71] Yet the strategy they have rejected is a biblical strategy. The evangelicals need to bow to that authoritative Scripture, recognize that separatism is scriptural, and reorder the practice of their ministries. Henry tacitly admits that the strategy of infiltration has failed. We must observe that the reason the strategy has failed is that it is contrary to the Bible's teaching.

This truth can be illustrated by the doctor who prepares to deliver a baby. On April 19, 1965, I watched the obstetrician scrub before he delivered our son Jim. He asked me to talk to him while he prepared. We stood in St. Mary's Hospital in Rochester,

Minnesota, while he followed the posted regulations. For four minutes he scrubbed from his hands to his elbows. Then he scrubbed the same way with another soap for another three minutes. He did not scrub in order to display his clean hands or to boast of their purity. His purpose was to minister to those who needed his skills and to aid in bringing new life into the world. A doctor cannot perform a delivery without sterilization. The sterilized obstetrician who does not deliver the baby leaves the mother and her baby in need. He is like the separated, fundamentalist pastor who goes weeks without attempting to win people to Christ, and who, of course, does not lead his people to evangelize either. The unsterilized physician who delivers the baby will greatly heighten the risks to the mother and her newborn infant. So is the New Evangelical who evangelizes while honoring and working with unbelieving, apostate ministers. Obstetrics and sterilization must, of necessity accompany each other. Evangelism and separatism are of equal necessity, inseparable companions.

May God grant that a new generation of pastors, evangelists, missionaries, Christian workers and laymen will determine to fervently declare to men that "now is the day of salvation" (II Cor. 6:2), militantly refuse to be "unequally yoked together with unbelievers" (II Cor. 6:14), and in purity seek to be "perfecting holiness in the fear of God" (II Cor. 7:1).

Notes

[1]Harold John Ockenga, Press Release, December 8, 1957, Boston, The Park Street Church. See Appendix B, pp. 117-19, for the full text of the press release.

[2]John Monroe Parker, interview by author, written notes, 18 December 1991. Dr. Parker provides some details about Graham becoming the spokesman for the New Evangelicalism. At the 1946 meeting of the National Association of Evangelicals in Chicago, Ockenga proposed to the Commission on Evangelism that an evangelist be recruited. The commission accepted the proposal and recommended it to the body. The general body of the NAE rejected the proposal at that time.

After Graham's famous 1949 crusade in Los Angeles, Ockenga, who had visited the crusade, became Graham's "chief counselor." Graham canceled his subsequent meetings, and his next crusade was in 1950 in Boston Garden. Ockenga's press release and subsequent history make it clear that Graham became the spokesman for the movement whether or not the NAE ever took formal action.

[3]"Is Evangelical Theology Changing?" *Christian Life,* March 1956, p. 2.

[4]W. E. Vine, *Vine's Expository Dictionary of New Testament Words* (McLean: MacDonald Publishing Co., n.d.), pp. 73-74.

[5]We understand Scripture to teach that the word *church* is used in two senses. Frederick James Moritz, "Church As Body," *Calvary Baptist Theological Journal,* Spring 1990, pp. 1-23, concludes that there is a "great," or so-called universal, church which is comprised of all believers from this age. This church is not yet functioning but is prospective. The reason it does not now function is that some of its members are in heaven, some on earth, and some are yet unborn. Hebrews 12:22-24 teaches that all born-again believers will meet in this "church of the firstborn" with Jesus in heaven. The ecclesiastical entity which functions on earth today is the local church. Therefore the New Testament instructions concerning ecclesiastical separation were and are given to local churches. As local churches cooperate together and work through associations of churches, evangelistic endeavors, and institutions such as colleges and mission agencies, these principles also apply. It is interesting to note, in the light of passages such as I Corinthians 3:17 and Ephesians 2:21 and 5:27, that the great, or universal, church will be perfected in holiness (and therefore completely separate from sin) in eternity.

[6]John Stewart Holland, "A Biblical Theology of Separation" (Ph.D. Dissertation, Bob Jones University, 1976), has done a massive work of cataloging Scripture on the subject of separation.

[7]E. H. Plumtre and T. Whitelaw, *Ezekiel,* vol. 12 of *The Pulpit Commentary,* ed. H.D.M. Spence and Joseph S. Excell (Grand Rapids: Eerdmans, 1962 reprint), p. 2.

[8]Jeremiah 51:45 ("My people, go ye out of the midst of her") is possibly an additional reference to which the II Corinthians passage may allude. Eberhard Nestle, ed. *Novum Testamentum Graece* (Stuttgart: Biblia P. W. B. 1961 edition), p. 466.

[9]Donald Grey Barnhouse, "One Church." *Eternity,* July 1958, p. 20 (emphasis Barnhouse's).

[10]Ernest Pickering, *Biblical Separation: The Struggle for a Pure Church* (Schaumburg: Regular Baptist Press, 1979), pp. 176-77, also offers a convincing refutation of this argument.

[11]James Thompson, *The Second Letter to the Corinthians,* vol. 9 of *The Living Word Commentary,* ed. Everett Ferguson (Austin: R. B. Sweet Co., Inc., 1970), p. 93.

[12]Warren W. Wiersbe, *The Bible Exposition Commentary* (Wheaton: Victor Books, 1989), 1:652.

[13]Henry Alford, *The Greek New Testament* (Cambridge: Deighton, Bell, and Co., 1877), 2:671.

[14]Douglas Groothuis, "Confronting the New Age," *Christianity Today,* 13 January 1989, p. 36.

[15]Ibid.

[16]Ibid., p. 37.

[17]R.C.H. Lenski, *The Interpretation of I and II Corinthians* (Minneapolis: Augsburg Publishing House, 1963), p. 1079.

[18]The realm of the believer is the realm of Christ and the realm of the unbeliever is the realm of Belial (II Cor. 6:15). This term "Belial" comes from a Hebrew word meaning "worthless." It came to be used as it is in this passage, of Satan. Charles Hodge, *Commentary on the Second Epistle to the Corinthians* (Grand Rapids: Eerdmans, n.d.), p. 169.

[19]Lenski, pp. 1080-84.

[20]Nestle, p. 466.

[21]Thompson, 9:94.

[22]A. T. Robertson, *Word Pictures in the New Testament* (Grand Rapids: Baker Book House, 1931), 4:237.

[23]Ibid.

[24]Ibid.

[25]Philip Edgcumbe Hughes, *Paul's Epistle to the Corinthians,* The New International Commentary on the New Testament, ed. Ned B. Stonehouse (Grand Rapids: Eerdmans, 1962), p. 253.

[26]Hodge, p. 172.

[27]Lenski, p. 1090.

[28]Ibid., p. 1091.

[29]Robertson, 4:238.

[30]Ibid.

[31]William F. Arndt and F. Wilbur Gingrich, *A Greek-English Lexicon of the New Testament* (Chicago: University of Chicago Press, 1957), p. 302.

[32]Alexander Balmain Bruce, "Matthew" in *The Expositor's Greek New Testament,* ed. W. Robertson Nicoll (Grand Rapids: Eerdmans, 1976 reprint), 1:133.

[33]Arndt and Gingrich, p. 404.

[34]Ibid., p. 202.

[35]Ibid., p. 420.

[36]Jac. J. Müller, *The Epistles of Paul to the Philippians and Philemon* (Grand Rapids: Eerdmans, 1955), p. 107.

[37]Arndt and Gingrich, p. 420.

[38]Ibid., p. 23.

[39]Robertson, 4:606.

[40]Joseph Henry Thayer, *Greek-English Lexicon of the New Testament* (Grand Rapids: Zondervan, 1979), p. 130.

[41]Arndt and Gingrich, p. 669.

[42]W. E. Vine, *Exposition of the Epistles to Timothy* (London: Pickering and Inglis, 1925), p. 13.

[43]Homer A. Kent, Jr., *The Pastoral Epistles* (Chicago: Moody Press, 1958), p. 148.

[44]Kent, p. 149.

[45]Donald Guthrie, *The Pastoral Epistles* (Grand Rapids: Eerdmans, 1957), p. 111.

[46]Guthrie, p. 111.

[47]William Hendricksen, *Exposition of the Pastoral Epistles,* New Testament Commentary (Grand Rapids: Baker Book House, 1957), pp. 263-64.

[48]Patrick Fairbairn, *Pastoral Epistles* (Reprint ed., Minneapolis: Klock and Klock Christian Publishers, Inc., 1980), p. 347.

[49]Hendricksen, p. 266.

[50]Wiersbe, 2:248. It must be noted that Wiersbe is not always consistent with this advice. R. L. Sumner, in a review of Wiersbe's *A Basic Library for Bible Students* in *The Sword of the Lord* (20 November 1981, p. 6), shows that Wiersbe consistently recommends the writings of liberals such as William Barclay, Elton Trueblood, Ralph W. Sockman, and Helmut Thieleke.

[51]M. R. Vincent, *Word Studies in the New Testament* (MacDill AFB, Fla.: MacDonald Publishing Company, n.d.), 2:1061.

[52]Harold J. Ockenga, *The Epistles to the Thessalonians, Proclaiming the New Testament* (Grand Rapids: Baker Book House, 1962), 3:136-37.

[53]Ockenga, p. 137.

[54]Ibid., p. 138.

[55]Ibid., p. 140.

[56]John E. Ashbrook, *Axioms of Separation* (Mentor, Ohio: "Here I Stand" Books, n.d.), pp. 5-6.

[57]*Know Your Roots: Evangelicalism Yesterday, Today, and Tomorrow* (Madison: 2100 Productions, 1991), videocassette.

[58]Ibid.

[59]Ibid.

[60]Ibid.

[61]Ibid.

[62]Ibid.

[63]Ockenga, Press Release, p. 2.

[64]*Know Your Roots* videocassette.

[65]Ibid.

[66]Ibid.

[67]Ibid.

[68]Ibid.

[69]William E. Ashbrook, *Evangelicalism, The New Neutralism* (Mentor, Ohio: John E. Ashbrook, 9th printing, n.d.), pp. 9-17.

[70]Pickering, pp. 141-55. See also Ernest Pickering, *The Tragedy of Compromise: The Origin and Impact of the New Evangelicalism* (Greenville, S.C.: Bob Jones University Press, 1994).

[71]*Know Your Roots* videocassette.

4

SEPARATION FROM A CHRISTIAN BROTHER

As long as biblical separation is discussed on a theoretical level, many Christians do not question its importance. When separation is applied in practice to people and institutions they know, however, some believers bristle. They ask challenging but thorny questions. Should local churches and believers ever separate themselves from other local churches and believers who disobey Scripture or do not practice biblical separation? If one is to separate from a brother, by what biblical standard is the decision to separate to be made? The Bible provides clear answers to these questions.

Positions Advocated

This issue was apparently first raised by those who embraced New Evangelicalism. Donald Grey Barnhouse seems to have been the first to advocate the position that separation from a Christian brother is not taught in Scripture. In September of 1957 he wrote, "The Bible teaches separation from individual apostates who deny the deity of the Lord Jesus Christ. But many believers do not know [that] . . . nowhere does the Bible suggest that believers separate from each other because of differences in the interpretation of even important doctrines. The only grounds for separation between believers is moral."[1]

Barnhouse also delivered a famous and controversial address at the Fifth Student Missionary Convention of the Inter-Varsity Christian Fellowship in December of 1957. The unedited transcript of that address was later published in *Eternity*. Barnhouse raised the issue under discussion and gave a slight variation of the position he had taken earlier that year: "Personally I came, within the last half dozen years, to the conclusion that if any man truly believes that Jesus Christ is Lord and the Savior of the world, that I must have fellowship with him. I may not be separated from him because I don't like him personally; I may not be separated from him because I think he has some queer doctrine."[2] Barnhouse went on to describe how that position resulted in his becoming a television spokesman for the National Council of Churches "and got me mixed up with Seventh Day Adventists and Pentecostalists."[3]

If this position were advocated only by Barnhouse, citing it now would be like "beating a dead horse." However, others have advocated that same position to the present hour. It is noteworthy that whereas those who first espoused the position were openly in the New Evangelical camp, some who currently hold it identify themselves as fundamentalists. Jack Van Impe, for instance, affirms that at least two New Testament passages (I Cor. 5:1-11; II Thess. 3:6-14) teach separation from believers but insists that these passages deal only with moral turpitude or idleness.[4] He states, "Basically then, two texts have been used to create the greatest mistrust of brothers in the history of Christendom. This tragedy exists because a platform and position has been built upon an erroneous interpretation of God's Word."[5]

Tim Lee is another who holds that Scripture does not teach separation from Christian brothers. He wrote to one fundamentalist leader, "Please allow me to share this thought with you. Maybe it isn't scripturally sound, let's see what you think. I maintain that separation from believers with whom we disagree is a decision made totally by man. All of the above mentioned doctrines originate with God. In other words, man had nothing to do with the virgin birth, the resurrection, the blood atonement, etc. But when it comes to second and third degree separation, as you and others promote, there is no clear biblical rule or verse to follow."[6]

Because the term "secondary separation" has appeared in this discussion and will appear again, we must say that we reject that term with the implication that separation from a fellow Christian is different from, or of lesser importance than, any other form of separation. Holiness is the foundation of separation, and this chapter will show that if separation between brethren becomes necessary, the ground of that separation will be principles based upon the holiness of God. As personal separation cannot be divorced from ecclesiastical separation because both are the outgrowth of God's holiness, so separation from disobedient brethren cannot be divorced from ecclesiastical separation for the same reason. We should reiterate at this point that the purpose of this work is to explain and defend the scriptural position concerning God's holiness and Christian separation, not to launch a malicious attack against those who hold the opposing view. The reason for citing these individuals is merely to demonstrate that numerous persons have held and advocated this opposing position from the 1950s to the present. During that same period of time, however, other Christians have promoted the biblical view that believers must separate from fellow believers under certain circumstances. Walter Handford answered Barnhouse shortly after Barnhouse's address at Urbana, saying, "In Galatians 5:19-21 the Bible links together as works of the flesh idolatry, witchcraft, and heresies, which are doctrinal matters, with adultery, murder, and other obvious sins of behaviour. Wrong teaching about the resurrection (evil speaking) corrupts good manners (behaviour) as I Corinthians 15:33 shows. . . . Moral behaviour lapses and doctrinal lapses cannot be divided as neatly as Dr. Barnhouse teaches."[7]

Many other Christians have also affirmed that separation from brethren is a duty in certain situations. Rolland McCune, for instance, holds the same position, affirming that "the Bible teaches separation from Christians who are doctrinally careless or who are content to walk with those who deny the faith."[8] Ernest Pickering has demonstrated that there are several instances where local churches and believers are to withhold fellowship from other believers. He cites instances such as "an act of [church] discipline, . . . refusal to allow Charismatics to have membership or ministry in a school or church, [and] . . . refusal to cooperate in ecumenical evangelistic crusades."[9] He states, "We believe that God's Word does give us direction. There are some solid reasons supporting the concept of refusing cooperative fellowship to fellow believers who are compromising in vital areas."[10]

Robert P. Lightner also weighs in for the view that there are times that brethren must separate. He says, "A more difficult biblical truth for many to accept and obey is separation from Christian brethren who persist in walking in disobedience."[11] Similarly, Robert Delnay deals with the question of those who cooperate with unbelievers and the separatist's position and attitude toward them: "On the one hand, we grieve over their disobedience and, I trust, we grieve without personal animosity. But when it comes to platform cooperation, we cannot yoke with them."[12]

The Bible faculty of Bob Jones University enumerates four situations in which such separation may be necessary: from a church member who persists in worldly living, from a brother who follows a false teacher, from a "Christian leader who refuses to take action against those who have been disobedient," or from a professing Christian who becomes divisive.[13] They echo Delnay, saying, "Concerned Christians have to break fellowship with heavy hearts, and even then there is still the hope that true repentance will be the result."[14]

It is clear that there are two clearly defined positions in the debate. We will not settle the matter by aligning scholars, commentators, and Christian leaders on one side of the issue or the other. Instead, we must examine the biblical evidence and answer the question: Does the Bible teach that separation from brethren is ever necessary? A second question logically follows: If such separation is necessary, are the grounds for it moral only, or both moral and doctrinal? Third, how far does the separatist go in his separation? Where does he draw the lines of separation? This chapter intends to demonstrate that Scripture teaches separation from believers on both moral and doctrinal grounds and that Scripture also sets certain standards for that separation. This study also intends to be objective in examining the scriptural evidence and attempts to be kind in disagreeing with those who hold the opposing view.

Applicable Scriptures

Matthew 18:15-17

The Lord Jesus gave these instructions to His disciples and intended them to be applied in the local churches after their establishment: "Moreover if thy brother shall trespass against thee, go and tell him his fault between thee and him alone: if he shall hear thee, thou hast gained thy brother. But if he will not hear thee, then take with thee one or two more, that in the mouth of two or three witnesses every word may be established. And if he neglect to hear them, tell it unto the church: but if he neglect to hear the church, let him be unto thee as an heathen man and a publican" (Matt. 18:15-17).

Several truths are apparent from this passage. First, Jesus was dealing with a problem arising between brethren. Second, the matters with which Christ dealt were neither petty nor trivial. The matters which were either to be rectified by the brothers involved or else dealt with by church discipline were sin. The word *trespass* (v. 15) is the verb ἁμαρτάνω (*hamartanō*), which is the standard New Testament word for "sin."[15] The use of the aorist tense of the verb "indicates a specific act of sinning,"[16] and speaks of a sin committed by one Christian against another. If the offended brother cannot gain reconciliation privately with the offending brother, then one or two others are to be brought in on the matter for counsel. If the second attempt fails, the offense is to be taken to the church, again with the aim of reconciling the brothers involved. If the sinning brother will not hear the church, he is to be excluded from the fellowship of the church and regarded as an unsaved man. This is a case in which the New Testament teaches that separation between a local church and an erring brother is to occur. The biblical ground for that separation is sin, not some trite issue. Although Jesus does not specify the sin, neither does He exclude any class or classes of sin. The separation is to take place only as a last resort, when repeated attempts at reconciliation have failed.

I Corinthians 5:1-11

The immediate occasion of Paul's instructions to the Corinthian church is the existence of fornication.[17] The man involved has "his father's wife" (v. 1). This language is used to describe the man's stepmother.[18] The man apparently was married to his stepmother, since "the uniform use of the phrase to have a woman in the New Testament . . . always means, to marry."[19] Hodge also concludes from II Corinthians 7:12 that the man's father was still alive.[20] Paul commands the church to remove the offending member from the fellowship of the church and deliver him "to Satan for the destruction of the flesh" (v. 5). The Corinthian church was, in this case of gross immorality, to separate itself from the sinning member.

Expanded Application

After Paul deals with this specific case which demanded his attention, he uses the occasion to establish a broader principle for the Corinthian church and for local churches today: "I wrote unto you in an epistle not to company with fornicators: Yet not altogether with the fornicators of this world, or with the covetous, or extortioners, or with idolaters; for then must ye needs go out of the world. But now I have written unto you not to keep company, if any man that is called a brother be a fornicator, or covetous, or an idolater, or a railer, or a drunkard, or an extortioner; with such a one, no, not to eat" (I Cor. 5:9-11).

Paul charges the Corinthians to act on a specific situation, which is the discipline of a professing Christian living in fornication. He then expands that specific situation into a broad principle, extending the command to separate from a disobedient brother to six classes of sinning believers. In addition to the immoral brother ("fornicator"), Paul instructs the Corinthian church to exclude from its fellowship the covetous Christian (covetousness being "committed by one who has all he needs but is greedy to gain even more"[21]); the "idolater"; the "railer," or "abusive person"[22]; the "drunkard"; and the "extortioner" (who is a "robber . . . better, swindler"[23]).

The command to exclude the idolater is of particular importance to this discussion. The idolater, simply put, was one who participated in idol worship. Hodge notes in addition that "eating sacrifices within the precincts of a temple was an act of heathen worship as much as partaking of the Lord's Supper is an act of Christian worship. And yet some of the Corinthians did not hesitate to eat of the heathen sacrifices under those circumstances, 10:14-22."[24] The separation from a disobedient brother in this instance is on doctrinal as well as moral grounds. Immorality was practiced in idolatry to be sure, but the act of participating in heathen worship was an act of embracing a false, anti-God, devilish religion (I Cor. 10:20-21).

Paul forbids such worship in I Corinthians 5:11 and 10:19-22, and this is precisely the point of his command in II Corinthians 6:14–7:1, where he forbids the unequal yoke. Paul not only teaches the church not to be unequally yoked with unbelievers (II Cor. 6:14), but he also commands the church to separate from the brother who persists in maintaining that unequal yoke (I Cor. 5:11). In fact, the apostle commands the church to separate itself from the unequally yoked brother *before* he commands it to separate from unbelievers. With all due respect for those who have adopted a different position, it must be stated that this passage commands separation from a disobedient brother on both theological and moral grounds.

In short, I Corinthians 5 demonstrates that the line of separation from the disobedient brother is exactly the same as it is from the unbeliever. The local church is to separate itself not only from an unbeliever but also from the believer who remains unequally yoked with an unbeliever. To be obedient to God's Word, a local church must not be yoked in cooperation, fellowship, organization, or evangelistic endeavor with unbelievers. Should a fellow Christian insist on remaining unequally yoked in such a way, the local church or believer must separate from him.

Holiness and Separation

Paul's teaching in this passage is perfectly consistent with the rest of Scripture's teaching on separation. The foundation of personal separation is God's holiness. Of the six sins named in I Corinthians 5:11, three (covetousness, fornication, and drunkenness) are directly named in chapters 4 and 5 of Ephesians (a passage which was examined in Chapter 3). "Railing" is similar to the statements on the believer's speech in Ephesians 4:29. The swindler is a thief (Eph. 4:28). The instruction about the idolater is comparable to the command against the unequal yoke in II Corinthians 6:14. Every sin which Paul deals with in I Corinthians 5 is related to God's holiness in another New Testament passage. The local church is to separate itself from the believer who continually practices gross sin, which is an affront to the holiness of God and thus a reflection on the testimony of the church. Even so, separation from a disobedient brother is not to be eagerly sought, and the restoration of the brother is to be the primary aim. When separation from a brother is necessary, the scriptural dividing line is consistent with the holiness of God, and the division, however reluctantly made, must be made along those lines of holiness. The local church is to be holy in doctrine and lifestyle.

II Thessalonians 3:6-15

This passage of Scripture is hotly debated. There is no controversy, however, about the primary teaching of the passage. In verses 7-13, Paul instructs the Thessalonian church concerning those who had fallen into the consistent habit of not working. They were "loafers."[25] Paul had previously spoken to this church concerning the individual's responsibility to work (I Thess. 4:6-7, 11-12).[26] He had further told them to "warn them that are unruly" (I Thess. 5:14). Some of those disorderly brethren had continued in their practice, and now Paul was forced to tell the church to separate itself from them and to admonish them in the hope that they would repent and be restored to the fellowship. In the verses which command the action to discipline the disorderly brethren and separate from them, Paul says, "Now we command you, brethren, in the name of our Lord Jesus Christ, that ye withdraw yourselves from every brother that walketh disorderly, and not after the tradition which he received of us. . . . And if any man obey not our word by this epistle, note that man, and have no company with him, that he may be ashamed. Yet count him not as an enemy, but admonish him as a brother" (II Thess. 3:6, 14-15).

These verses speak plainly about the separation of the local church from a disobedient Christian. The verses are equally clear that the separation in this instance is on moral or ethical grounds. The brother from whom the church separates is stubbornly persisting in a lifestyle which is contrary to the holiness of God. The point of contention is whether this passage applies only to separation from the disobedient brother who will not work or whether the verses in question apply to a broader issue as well.

Context of the Passage

The context of the passage reaches back to the situation with which Paul first dealt in I Thessalonians 4. The use of the word *tradition* (II Thess. 3:6) also requires an examination in its context. The word is used by Paul earlier, in II Thessalonians 2:15. This word means "a giving over which is done by word of mouth or in writing."[27] Hiebert points out that it is used in three senses in the New Testament. It is used of the Jewish traditions (Mark 7:3-9; Matt. 15:2-6); of the Gnostic heresy (Col. 2:8); and "the third type of tradition in Scripture, the true God-given gospel message."[28] This was the basis of Paul's exhortation "Therefore, brethren, stand fast, and hold the traditions which ye have been taught, whether by word, or our epistle" (II Thess. 2:15).

The traditions which they were to hold were not manmade, but rather they were Paul's inscripturated writings. He told them to hold to what they had been taught in the Word of God. In the light of that greater context, they were to "withdraw . . . from every brother that walketh disorderly, and not after the tradition which he received of us" (II Thess. 3:6). The church was also commanded to separate from those who "obey not our word by this epistle" (II Thess. 3:14).

Interpretation of the Passage

This passage clearly teaches separation from brethren in Christ who are openly and willfully disobedient to the written, revealed Word of God and is not limited in its application to the lazy brother only. Consider first the nature of the tradition. Paul tells the church to "hold the traditions" that they had received "whether by word, or our epistle" (II Thess. 2:15). That tradition would be *all* of what Paul wrote in I Thessalonians, and the teaching on work is *part* of that revealed, inspired epistle. Paul then focuses the word *tradition* on the loafer with whom he had dealt in I Thessalonians 4. Because he does not walk "after the tradition" (II Thess. 3:6) and does not "obey . . . our word by this epistle" (II Thess. 3:14), the church is to separate itself from him. Common sense leads to the conclusion that the same action should be taken concerning one who was flagrantly immoral, heretical in reference to the Lord's return, or continually disobedient in reference to other matters with which Paul deals in these two epistles. Bruce Compton notes, "By application, any conscious violation of a specific command given to them by the apostle would qualify the offender for the same discipline directed in verse 6."[29]

Consider also the consistency of Paul's logic. In I Corinthians 5 he begins with one issue, fornication, and expands it to a principle which demands separation from disobedient brethren in five other situations as well. In II Thessalonians he begins with the principle of inscripturated tradition and proceeds to the specific case of the brother who refuses to work. He then expands that specific case back into the broader principle of separation—"if any man obey not our word by this epistle" (II Thess. 3:14), whatever that word in the epistle may be. In both passages Paul deals both with principle and specific application. Just as it would be illogical to limit the I Corinthians 5 passage to the specific instance of fornication, so it also flies in the face of logic to limit II Thessalonians 3 to the specific instance which is obvious and ignore the principle upon which it is based. This is the same trap into which Barnhouse fell when he tried to say that II Corinthians 6 dealt only with the heathen temples in Corinth and had nothing to do with unbelieving apostates in our present day.[30]

Consider finally how this position is consistent with the rest of Scripture. The believer should forsake sin because sin is contrary to God's holiness. The local church is to separate itself from theological unbelief because the doctrine and accompanying life-style of apostasy is contrary to God's holiness. When a brother's lifestyle or doctrine opposes the holiness of God, then the local church must also separate from that brother.

Titus 3:9-11

This passage apparently deals with a brother. Paul writes his letter to Titus to deal with church life and specifically to "set in order the things that are wanting, and ordain elders in every city" (Titus 1:5). In the conclusion of this epistle, Paul says, "But avoid foolish questions, and genealogies, and contentions, and strivings about the law; for they are unprofitable and vain. A man that is an heretick, after the first and second admonition reject: knowing that he that is such is subverted, and sinneth, being condemned of himself" (Titus 3:9-11).

The key issue is to understand what Scripture means by the word "heretic." The Greek word αἱρετικός (*hairetikos*) conveys the idea "schismatic, factious, a follower of false doctrine."[31] Vine explains that it speaks of "especially a self-willed opinion which is substituted for submission to the power of the truth, and leads to division and the formation of sects."[32] Paul thus identifies the divisive man who, after the pattern of Acts 20:30 and III John 9, seeks for prominence in order to gain a following. Barnes notes that this heretic may form sects and parties on some points of doctrine on which he differs from others, or on some custom, religious rite or peculiar practice; he may make some unimportant matter a ground of distinction from his brethren, and may refuse to have fellowship with them and endeavor to set up a new organization.[33] The heretic is, in other words, one who promotes a peculiar doctrine and is divisive in doing it. Wiersbe points out that heresy is one of the works of the flesh (Gal. 5:20).[34] After giving two warnings, the believer and the church are to reject the divisive heretic.

Galatians 5:19-21

Scripture lists the works of the flesh in this passage: "Now the works of the flesh are manifest, which are these; adultery, fornication, uncleanness, lasciviousness, idolatry, witchcraft, hatred, variance, emulations, wrath, strife, seditions, heresies, envyings, murders, drunkenness, revellings, and such like: of the which I tell you before, as I have also told you in time past, that they which do such things shall not inherit the kingdom of God" (Gal. 5:19-21).

Very little needs to be said about this passage. Handford long ago noted, "The Bible links together as works of the flesh idolatry, witchcraft and heresies, which are doctrinal matters, with adultery, murder, and other obvious sins of behaviour."[35] Both doctrinal and moral matters are works of the flesh, and Scripture teaches that walking in the Spirit gives victory over both (Gal. 5:16). It should be no wonder that Christians who seek to obey God are taught to separate from disobedient believers who flagrantly indulge in sins of either kind.

Observations

Several observations should be made as we consider the biblical material.

Attitude

The last chapter of this book will be devoted to the separatist's spirit. At this point it should be clear that Scripture gives instructions to go privately and with one or two others before making a matter public (Matt. 18:15-17). Believers are told to view the transgressor as a brother in Christ, not an adversary, and they are to work for his restoration (II Thess. 3:14-15). Scripture commands repeated attempts to reconcile even the schismatic (Titus 3:10), and meek, spiritual Christians are to restore the brother who falls into the sins of the flesh (Gal. 5:19–6:2). A believer must exercise patience, and restoration—not separation—is the goal. Separation is the last resort. Separatists, rightly zealous for purity in doctrine and association, are still bound by these biblical obligations. There is no scriptural justification for hasty separation which is not preceded by repeated attempts to reconcile estranged brethren and to restore the erring brother.

Types of Offenses

Different offenses apparently are to be treated differently. Both I Corinthians 5 and II Thessalonians 3 command separation from the erring Christian. Yet in I Corinthians 5 the offender is to be completely cut off whereas in II Thessalonians 3 he is to be encouraged.[36]

Unanswered Questions

This study has sought to identify a biblical standard for separation from brethren where others have said that none exists. It has identified certain standards that Scripture sets down. This study makes no presumption of having answered all the questions or of solving all the problems involved. Lightner wisely observes, "How far removed from the original offender should one carry the matter of separation? Specific answers to these questions are not given in the Bible. Each case it would seem, therefore, must be decided on its own merits. In making such a decision a believer must be sure he does not disobey any clearly stated teachings of Scripture."[37]

Conclusion

An objective study of the New Testament leads first to the conclusion that the New Testament teaches that there are times when local churches and believers must reluctantly take the action of separating themselves from other believers. The purpose of such separation is purity. The local church specifically is to take the extreme action of separation from a disobedient brother when necessary in order to preserve its purity of life and testimony. Restoration is always to be the goal, and the act of separation is to be the last resort.

The second conclusion is that the New Testament also sets clear standards for that separation when it must be made. Those standards include the following:

1. *The sinning brother*—Sin by one brother against another about which the sinning brother will not be reconciled (Matt. 18:15-17).

2. *The immoral brother*—Moral sins that the sinning brother continues to practice. These are fornication, covetousness, railing, drunkenness, and extortion (I Cor. 5:11).

3. *The unequally yoked brother*—The doctrinal, or theological, error of idolatry, or being unequally yoked with unbelievers (I Cor. 5:11; II Cor. 6:14).

4. *The lazy brother*—The sin of laziness in which the brother will not work for a living (II Thess. 3:6-15).

5. *The disobedient brother*—Open disobedience to Scripture (II Thess. 2:15; 3:6-14).

6. *The heretical brother*—Heresy, or deviant doctrine, that is promoted out of self-willed divisiveness (Titus 3:10).

The third conclusion is an observation. Like the commands to ecclesiastical separation, these instructions are given to local churches and deal with matters of the internal life and affairs of the church. Churches, pastors, and other leaders will need to apply these principles to situations of cooperation and fellowship between churches, or between churches and service agencies.

The fourth conclusion is that separation from brethren, like personal separation and ecclesiastical separation, has the holiness of God as its foundation. Most of the sins and errors which ultimately demand separation are stated in Scripture to be contrary to God's holiness.

A fifth conclusion is that pastors must provide responsible spiritual leadership (Acts 20:28)[38] to the churches they lead. They must protect the local churches they pastor from unbiblical alliances and compromises.

Sixth, this study should lead pastors and local churches to a sober examination of the New Testament teaching on church discipline. God intends the local churches to preserve their purity.

Seventh, agencies and institutions that serve local churches must prayerfully apply these principles of separation to their ministries. Associations of churches, mission agencies, publishing houses, Christian colleges and seminaries, and other such organizations are also responsible to be consistent in obedience to the principles delineated in Scripture.

Another conclusion is that those who espouse biblical separatism must practice a consistent standard. It is folly to emphasize ecclesiastical separation, to warn against New Evangelicalism, and to encourage pastors to minister without compromise and at the same time to overlook moral failures. Preachers in this materialistic age should compare the volume of the Bible's teaching about covetousness to the amount of their preaching against the same sin!

We must also conclude that separatists must be careful to be consistent with Scripture in their separation, and that means that they must not go beyond the biblical guidelines. The common argument against separation from brethren is that "there is no place to stop." That is clearly a smokescreen raised by those who oppose the biblical position. Separatists need to exercise discernment that they are on solid biblical grounds when they practice separation.

A word is in order to a generation of young preachers. Many of the militant leaders who stood for biblical separation are in glory or advancing in years. Younger men who have not had to fight battles may wonder why those leaders stood where they did. Many of the younger generation are searching for a frame of reference. Bixby makes a fair plea for answers. Speaking of secondary separation, which he defines as "separating from another Christian who is somewhat less separated than you are,"[39] he states, "It may be that the practice is correct but, if this generation is going to live in Biblical balance, then the exegetically defensible support for such a practice needs to be presented. Again, considering the importance of unity, the decision to separate must be supported by clear Biblical principle or risk divine censure for being illegitimately factious."[40]

This study has endeavored to make a contribution toward providing those answers, both in relation to separation from brethren and in the larger context as well. A plea must also be directed to those who identify themselves as fundamentalists but who in the past have not agreed that Scripture teaches separation from brethren. This study is not an attack on you. Those who have been quoted have either put their ideas into the public domain or granted permission to be quoted. This study has endeavored to treat them kindly, fairly, and objectively. Please carefully examine the evidence which the Bible presents. The same Book which teaches separation from false teachers and false doctrine also teaches separation from unequally yoked and otherwise disobedient believers.

Notes

[1]Donald Grey Barnhouse, "Thanksgiving and Warning," *Eternity,* September 1957, p. 9.

[2]Donald Grey Barnhouse, "One Church," *Eternity,* July 1958, p. 20.

[3]Ibid.

[4]Jack Van Impe, *Heart Disease In Christ's Body* (Royal Oak, Mich.: Jack Van Impe Ministries, 1984), pp. 156-61.

[5]Ibid., p. 153.

[6]Tim Lee to R. L. Hymers, 24 May 1990; used with Lee's permission.

[7]Walter E. Handford, "Is Dr. Barnhouse Right?" *Sword of the Lord,* 24 January 1958, p. 11. We must note that Handford's position differs from the position we take in this book. This chapter concludes that believers must refuse to cooperate with other believers over several issues, including doctrinal defection and moral impurity, which were the subject of the debate in the 1957 and 1958 articles written by Barnhouse and Handford. We conclude that believers must also refuse to fellowship and cooperate with believers who are unequally yoked with unbelievers. Handford stated his position: "My touchstone for whom I would use in my pulpit must go primarily to doctrine—basically primary doctrine" (Letter to Fred Moritz, 28 February 1992, p. 2). Although Handford would separate from an erring brother over doctrine or moral impurity, his position allows him to work with believers who cooperate with unbelievers. We believe that Scripture teaches otherwise.

[8]Rolland McCune, *Ecclesiastical Separation* (Detroit: Detroit Baptist Theological Seminary, n.d.), p. 4.

[9]Ernest Pickering, *Should We Ever Separate From Christian Brethren?* (Minneapolis: Central Press, n.d.), p. 3.

[10]Ibid., p. 4.

[11]Robert P. Lightner, "A Biblical Perspective on False Doctrine," *Bibliotheca Sacra,* January-March 1985, p. 20.

[12]Robert Delnay, "Ecclesiastical Separation," *Faith Pulpit,* June-August 1987, p. 2.

[13]Bible Faculty of Bob Jones University, *Biblical Separation* (Greenville, S.C.: Bob Jones University Press, 1980), pp. 13-14.

[14]Ibid., p. 13.

[15]William F. Arndt and F. Wilbur Gingrich, *A Greek-English Lexicon of the New Testament* (Chicago: University of Chicago Press, 1957), p. 41.

[16]R.C.H. Lenski, *The Interpretation of St. Matthew's Gospel* (Minneapolis: Augsburg Publishing House, 1964 printing), p. 698.

[17]G. G. Findlay, "St. Paul's First Epistle to the Corinthians," Vol. 2 of *The Expositor's Greek New Testament,* ed. W. Robertson Nicoll (Grand

Rapids: Eerdmans, 1983 reprint), p. 807, states that "πορνεία [porneia] signifies any immoral sexual relation whether including (as in Matt. v.32) or distinguished from (Matt. xv.19) μοιχεία [mocheia]."

[18]Paul R. Van Gorder, The Church Stands Corrected (Wheaton: Victor Books, 1976), p. 23.

[19]Charles Hodge, An Exposition of the First Epistle to the Corinthians (Grand Rapids: Eerdmans, 1974 reprint), p. 81.

[20]Ibid.

[21]Van Gorder, p. 30.

[22]Arndt and Gingrich, p. 480.

[23]Ibid., p. 108.

[24]Hodge, p. 90.

[25]D. Edmond Hiebert, The Thessalonian Epistles (Chicago: Moody Press, 1982 edition), p. 339.

[26]R.C.H. Lenski, The Interpretation of St. Paul's First Epistle to the Thessalonians (Minneapolis: Augsburg Publishing House, 1964 printing), p. 312, holds, as do "the majority of the commentators," that Paul is dealing in I Thessalonians 4:6 with "honest and unselfish business dealing and does not continue the admonition against sexual sins." This interpretation does not minimize the seriousness of immoral conduct. It does stress the importance of integrity in business dealings. It also links Paul's teaching on work (I Thess. 4:6, 11-12) to the holiness of God (I Thess. 4:3, 7). It should be noted that the passage in chapters 4 and 5 of Ephesians, which was examined extensively in Chapter 3, also links honesty and integrity in work to God's holiness (Eph. 4:28). In order to reflect God's holiness, the believer is not to defraud his brother in business (I Thess. 4:6) nor to steal (Eph. 4:28). He is to work honestly to maintain a good testimony and to provide for his own needs (I Thess. 4:11). His honest work will also enable him to give to others in need (Eph. 4:28).

[27]Joseph Henry Thayer, Greek English Lexicon of the New Testament (Grand Rapids: Zondervan, 1970), p. 481.

[28]Hiebert, p. 326.

[29]R. Bruce Compton, "2 Thessalonians 3:6-15 and Biblical Separation," The Sentinel, Fall 1988, p. 2.

[30]Barnhouse, "One Church," p. 20.

[31]Thayer, p. 16.

[32]W. E. Vine, Vine's Expository Dictionary of New Testament Words, McLean: MacDonald Publishing Company, n.d.), p. 557.

[33]Albert Barnes, Thessalonians-Philemon, Notes on the New Testament (Grand Rapids: Baker Book House, 1979 reprint), p. 287.

[34]Warren W. Wiersbe, *The Bible Exposition Commentary*, (Wheaton: Victor Books, 1989), 2:268.

[35]Handford, p. 11.

[36]Don W. Bixby, "Separation: In Search of Balance" (Unpublished term paper, Central Baptist Theological Seminary, 1990), pp. 9-12, has a helpful, detailed discussion of this question.

[37]Lightner, p. 21.

[38]Pickering, p. 7.

[39]Bixby, p. 29.

[40]Ibid.

5

THE SPIRIT OF THE SEPARATIST

Separation is a battle. When one takes a positive stand for holiness and truth, he embraces a cause that reflects God's nature. That cause also is contrary to every purpose of Satan. The separatist will have to identify false teachers and their doctrine. He will have to expose them and separate his ministry from them. Conflict with Satan and men whom he uses is inevitable. Bible believers will sometimes have to separate themselves with a heavy heart from brethren who are dear to them.

Such a conflict brings accompanying dangers. Separation and purity are a vital part of the ministry, but they are not all of the ministry. It is easy for the separatist to forget the other vital facets of the ministry. Ernest Pickering lists several dangers which lurk to harm the ministry of the separatist: "An improper spirit, . . . over-occupation with the issues, . . . uncontrolled suspicion, . . . a desire to dominate, . . . failure to see the larger picture, . . . caustic language, . . . public instead of private rebuke."[1] Paul Jackson also describes the tension that the biblical separatist experiences as he seeks to stand for truth. After describing the dangers of radicalism and a wrong attitude he says, "When we have great convictions, the natural tendency is for us to become rough and vehement. It is equally difficult, on the other hand, to manifest a gracious attitude and yet be strong. The tendency in the manifestation of grace is to compromise and be weak. Only in the Lord Jesus are these two things properly brought together in balance."[2]

The purpose of this chapter is to learn what the Bible teaches about the spirit of the separatist. It will challenge those who stand for biblical separation to let the Holy Spirit make their heart attitude what God says it ought to be.

Passion for Holiness

The first element of the separatist's spirit to consider must be a desire for holiness. This study has clearly demonstrated that separation is a part of the holiness of God. Let it be understood that separation is by no means all there is to God's holiness, but separation is one integral part of that holiness. Man's separation naturally flows from his understanding of God's holiness. Personal separation from the "former lusts" (I Pet. 1:14) of his old life comes as the Christian imitates the holiness of God (I Pet. 1:15-16). The separation of the local church from unbelievers comes from a desire to perfect holiness (II Cor. 6:14–7:1). The local church must also separate from erring believers when those believers offend God's holiness by tolerating and practicing sin in their lives (I Thess. 4:1-7; II Thess. 3:14-15).

One who understands this truth concludes that if the individual Christian and the local church will pursue holiness (Heb. 12:14), then the right kind of separation will follow. God's holiness, and the meaning of that holiness for mankind, permeates the Scriptures. Its depths can never be plumbed. One who studies and pursues holiness will come to a proper understanding of God and will properly balance biblical separation in his life and ministry.

Unwavering Militancy

The Christian who understands the Scripture's teaching about separation will never apologize for being militant in his defense of God's Word and in exposing those who deny it and work to destroy it. Jude exhorts his readers to "earnestly contend for the faith" (Jude 3). He spares nothing in describing the apostates and their moral and doctrinal corruption (Jude 4, 8, 10, 12-13, 16, 19). Paul was relentless and unapologetic in warning churches and preachers about false teachers. He exposed their true spiritual character (II Cor. 11:3-4, 13-15), named some of them by name (I Tim. 1:18-20; II Tim. 2:16-18), and—with tears—used stronger language than many today would dare to use in describing their lifestyle and their end (Phil. 3:17-19). Peter's language in II Peter 2 is equally plain as he describes the doctrine and character of these false teachers. John's commands to separation in II John 7-11 cannot be misunderstood. It is apparent that the apostles who were used of the Holy Spirit to write the New Testament never divided over the strategy of separation.

Previous generations of separatists battled error and stood for the Faith. Some fought unbelief in major denominations or conventions of churches, eventually leaving those organizations. Then came the battles over ecumenical evangelism and the division between fundamentalism and New Evangelicalism. Some present-day leaders were forced to leave former circles of fellowship because groups and organizations which once stood for separatism moved toward a nonseparatist position. These conflicts often cost dearly as men sacrificed financial security, positions of leadership, and personal friendships. That generation of men, many of whom are in heaven and some of whom are still on the scene, deserve the respect and gratitude of those who follow and enjoy the heritage of the churches and institutions they built. Those men were not perfect, however, and perhaps some were unduly harsh in their attitudes at times as they sought to do God's work. Because they were redeemed sinners, as are all believers, they may have exhibited other flaws in their ministries as well.

A dangerous tendency on the part of younger separatists today is to look at the weaknesses of the older generation and abandon or moderate the position they took because of these weaknesses. The present generation of preachers needs to realize that it too will leave a record of imperfection in its service for Christ. The shortcomings of former leaders do not justify forsaking or weakening the biblical position for which they fought. Men must be as militant as Jude, Paul, Peter, and John in the ministry of the Word. The Bible teaches militancy. Certainly the younger man today will not want to emulate whatever flaws are apparent in a leader. He should adopt the attitude which Paul asked his followers to adopt when he said, "Be ye followers of me, even as I also am of Christ" (I Cor. 11:1). The current generation should imitate the godliness of the past generation while not forsaking separation because of the human weaknesses of those leaders.

Zeal for Souls

The third part of the separatist's spirit should be a zeal to see people saved and a resulting consistency in evangelistic effort. This study has already identified passages in I Peter 2:9; II Corinthians

6:1-2; 6:14–7:1; and John 17:17-20 where evangelism and separation are linked. There is at least one other passage like it in Jude. After the exhortation to "earnestly contend for the faith" (v. 3) and the exposure of the apostates, Jude exhorts his readers, "And others save with fear, pulling them out of the fire; hating even the garment spotted by the flesh" (Jude 23). Evangelism and separation are inseparably joined in Scripture. The separatist must remember that separation is not an end in itself but a God-appointed means of proclaiming the gospel. Separation without evangelism is sterile, and the separatist has a God-given responsibility to consistently work for the salvation of souls around the world.

Perpetual Love for God

The Bible teaches the separatist that he must maintain his love relationship with his God. Jude's command is explicit: "But ye, beloved, building up yourselves on your most holy faith, praying in the Holy Ghost, keep yourselves in the love of God, looking for the mercy of our Lord Jesus Christ unto eternal life" (Jude 20-21).

These verses contain the command to "keep yourselves in the love of God." A warm-hearted relationship with the Lord must be perpetually preserved by the believer. This command is given to those who are to be the contenders for the Faith. Separatists must be spiritual Christians who walk with God. It is especially important to note that the loss of this love relationship is a clear and present danger to the separatist. The church at Ephesus was a separatist church which exposed false apostles, but Christ rebuked it, saying, "Thou hast left thy first love" (Rev. 2:4). The separatist needs to remember to preserve his place of communion with God, and he needs to fear leaving that first love.

God not only gives instruction to "keep yourselves in the love of God" (Jude 21), but He also teaches the Christian how to do it. The passage contains three participial phrases that modify the imperative: "*building* yourselves up on your most holy faith, *praying* in the Holy Ghost, . . . *looking* for the mercy of our Lord Jesus Christ unto eternal life" (Jude 20-21). The believer is to contend for the revealed faith, and he is to build himself up in that faith. The Word of God is that revealed faith which builds men (Acts 20:32). The Christian is also to pray and look for the return of Christ. By these three actions the believer keeps himself in the love of God.

Fruit of The Spirit

The New Testament directly associates with separation three virtues that are part of the fruit of the Holy Spirit in the believer's life (Gal. 5:22-23): love, gentleness, and meekness. They must characterize the attitude of the biblical separatist. When the believer "walk[s] in the Spirit" (Gal. 5:16), the Holy Spirit produces His fruit in the believer. Some of that fruit must be displayed in the attitude of the person who obeys God in the matter of separation.

Love

As the Holy Spirit leads up to the long passage in Ephesians 4:17–5:18 that deals with personal separation, He teaches that a mark of maturity in the Christian life is "speaking the truth in love" (Eph. 4:15). Paul unequivocally speaks the truth in the following verses, but he does so with love for his readers and a desire that they lead Spirit-filled lives. The axiom of Ephesians 4:15 is demonstrated in his words in the following section. He also exhorts them to "walk in love" (Eph. 5:2). The Christian who loves God will hate sin and forsake it in the Spirit's power. These instructions accompany a militant, forceful passage which condemns sin and commands holiness in the Christian's life.

In another passage in which he refers to those who have "swerved" from Scripture (I Tim. 1:6), Paul states, "Now the end of the commandment is charity out of a pure heart, and of a good conscience, and of faith unfeigned" (I Tim. 1:5). Paul had instructed Timothy to rebuke some who had begun to teach false doctrine (I Tim. 1:3). He refers to that "charge" and says that love is the purpose of his "commandment" (v. 5) to rebuke them. Hiebert comments, "Their teaching produced strife and contention, but the charge of Timothy has as its aim the production of true and pure love."[3]

The preacher's aim must be to keep himself in the love of God and to build a love for God, for fellow Christians, and for all men in the hearts of his people. False doctrine, which detracts from that purpose, must be exposed and avoided (I Tim. 1:3-4).

Gentleness

Gentleness is to be another part of the separatist's attitude. In II Timothy 2:16-21, which has been previously discussed, Paul instructs Timothy to separate himself from false doctrine and to thus sanctify himself for God's use. Paul apparently taught Timothy to instruct those who were caught up in the false doctrine which Hymenaeus and Philetus propounded, saying, "And the servant of the Lord must not strive; but be gentle unto all men, apt to teach, patient" (II Tim. 2:24). Gentleness is required of the separated servant of the Lord who would seek to recover those caught up in false doctrine. In II Corinthians 10, Paul describes the spiritual warfare for the souls of men (vv. 3-6). He begins that militant passage by referring to the "meekness and gentleness of Christ" (v. 1). Twice he speaks of gentleness in passages where he is militant and separatistic.

Thayer describes gentleness as being "equitable, fair, mild."[4] Vine states that "it expresses that considerateness that looks 'humanely and reasonably at the facts of a case.' "[5] This attitude must characterize those who are separatists. It is never right to misrepresent those who deny the Word of God. If their doctrine is false it must be exposed and repudiated, but those who are caught up in false doctrine must be treated with that equity and fairness that constitute gentleness. This attitude is necessary because the separatist must hold out hope for the recovery of the one caught up in false doctrine (II Tim. 2:25-26). Scripture calls false doctrine "iniquity" and commands believers to separate from it (II Tim. 2:19), but they must seek the recovery of those from whom they separate over unholy doctrine. Hiebert speaks of the difficulty involved and the divine power necessary to effect such recovery: "The habit of the errorists to contradict the truth has made it hard for them even to listen to the truth. Only God can effect the change in them. He must 'give' it to them as a gift, using Timothy's efforts as the means to work the needed 'repentance' in them."[6]

This gentleness must also characterize the actions of separatists in their relationships with believers whom they perceive to be in error. This sense of equity demands that they go to them privately, before publicly exposing supposed error. This is a matter of biblical practice. These passages all deal with separation in the context of the local church, and in that context, separatists are to patiently seek to restore a brother before they separate from him. The same principle applies in a larger context. Before separatists expose a brother in a public forum, both common courtesy and biblical principle demand that they speak privately with him first. They may learn that a brother is not at all cooperating with a group whose meetings he may attend or whose resources he may use. To illustrate, every preacher uses books written by men with whom he has profound disagreement; doing so does not meant that he is "co-operating" with those authors. Churches may use educational materials from institutions with whom they do not agree and with whom they are not in cooperation. Separatists may learn that supposed compromise is not compromise at all, or that a brother has made an isolated mistake. Separatists must heed James's advice to be "swift to hear, slow to speak, slow to wrath" (James 1:19).

Meekness

Meekness is a part of the Spirit's fruit associated with separation. Paul refers to it along with gentleness in both II Corinthians 10:1 and II Timothy 2:24-25. He also states, "Brethren, if a man be overtaken in a fault, ye which are spiritual, restore such a one in the spirit of meekness; considering thyself, lest thou also be tempted" (Gal. 6:1).

Vine describes several important features that constitute meekness: "It is that temper of spirit in which we accept [God's] dealings with us as good, and therefore without disputing or resisting. . . . The meekness manifested by the Lord and commended to the believer is the fruit of power. . . . Described negatively, meekness is the opposite to self-assertiveness and self-interest. . . . It is not occupied with self at all."[7]

The separatist is to submit himself to God, and in a selfless, powerful manner stand against those who promote false doctrine. He is to exhibit this attitude in separating from the false teacher.

Patience

Another biblically mandated component of the separatist's spirit is patience. Paul tells Timothy that in separating from false teachers and instructing them he is to be "patient" (II Tim. 2:24). The word used is ἤπιος (*ēpios*), which is used only once in the New Testament.[8] It conveys the idea of "putting up with what is bad."[9] The believer must separate himself from false doctrine but be patient with the man who promotes the evil. This passage never condones compromise with false doctrine but repeatedly commands separation from it (II Tim. 2:16, 19, 21, 23). Paul identifies the false teachers by name and warns of the evil effect of their teaching (II Tim. 2:16-17). At the same time he requires patience with evil. He requires this in addition to gentleness and meekness as the servant of the Lord seeks the recovery of those who have fallen into error.

Prayerfulness

Scripture exhorts the separatist to diligence in praying. Prayer is one of the means by which the Christian keeps himself in the love of God (Jude 20). In I Timothy 1:18-20 Paul exhorts Timothy to a "good warfare" (v. 18) and warns him of those who have "concerning faith made shipwreck" (v. 19). He then states that the first priority in the life of the warrior for the Faith is "supplications, prayers, intercessions, and giving of thanks" (2:1). He says plainly that this must come "first of all"(v. 1). To protect oneself from false doctrine and to stand against it and for the Faith, prayer must be the preacher's priority.

Compassion

Paul's instructions to Timothy in II Timothy 2:16-25 imply a genuine compassion for the false teachers from whom Timothy had to separate. The clear instruction "yet count him not as an enemy, but admonish him as a brother" (II Thess. 3:15) makes it obvious that the separatist is to have a genuine concern for the erring brother from whom he must separate. Paul warned the Philippians about the "enemies of the cross of Christ" and said that he did it "even weeping." (Phil. 3:18). Perhaps Paul wept as he thought of the reproach brought on the cross by its enemies. Perhaps he wept for the enemies of the cross who had professed faith in Christ and now were "recreant followers of Christ."[10] His separation was accompanied by deep emotion, and was not harsh, unfeeling, and insensitive.

The Theme of Holiness

The theme of holiness weaves its way through this part of the study also. The separatist is to build himself upon his "most holy faith" (Jude 20). Meekness, gentleness, and love are required in the practice of separation. Those virtues are produced by the Holy Spirit in the believer and reflect God's holiness. The holiness of God is the foundation of all separation, and the separatist who has the right spirit will reflect the holiness of God in his practice of separation.

Conclusion

Perhaps the Bible constructs a model of the separatist which many who embrace separatism have never fully considered.

1. The separatist is a man who is first concerned about holiness. His separatism flows from an understanding of God's holiness and a desire to reflect that holiness in his personal life and in his ministry.

2. The separatist is a man of absolute militancy in a day when militancy is out of vogue.

3. The biblical separatist sees evangelism inseparably tied to separation and consistently works to get the gospel to lost people everywhere.

4. The separatist understands that purity of life and purity of doctrine go hand in hand and that he must maintain his daily walk with God.

5. The separatist realizes that in his militancy and refusal to compromise he must display the fruit of the Holy Spirit in his life. He knows that fruit is only produced in a life surrendered to the Spirit of God. Love, gentleness, and meekness mark his conduct.

6. The separatist knows that while he can have nothing to do with false doctrine and must not cooperate with false teachers in doing God's work, he must yet patiently instruct them and hope for their repentance.

7. The separatist makes prayer a priority as he wages his warfare.

8. The separatist has real compassion for those whose doctrine or lifestyle he must oppose.

May God's Spirit use His sword (Eph. 6:17) to convict a generation of separatists where they have failed and to make them militant in their stand and meek in their spirit!

Notes

[1] Ernest Pickering, *Biblical Separation: The Struggle for a Pure Church* (Schaumburg, Ill.: Regular Baptist Press, 1979), pp. 230-33.

[2] Paul R. Jackson, "The Positions, Attitudes, and Objectives of Biblical Separation" (Des Plaines, Ill.: General Association of Regular Baptist Churches, n.d.), p. 3.

[3] D. Edmond Hiebert, *First Timothy* (Chicago: Moody Press, 1957), p. 32.

[4] Joseph Henry Thayer, *Greek-English Lexicon of the New Testament* (Grand Rapids: Zondervan, 1970), p. 238.

[5] W. E. Vine, *Vine's Expository Dictionary of New Testament Words* (McLean: MacDonald Publishing Co., n.d.), pp. 484-85.

[6] D. Edmond Hiebert, *Second Timothy* (Chicago: Moody Press, 1958), pp. 78-79.

[7] Vine, p. 738.

[8] Walter Grundmann, "κακός," *Theological Dictionary of the New Testament,* ed. Gerhard Kittel (Grand Rapids: Eerdmans, 1974), 3:487.

[9] R.C.H. Lenski, *The Interpretation of St. Paul's Epistles to the Colossians, to the Thessalonians, to Timothy, to Titus and to Philemon* (Minneapolis: Augsburg Publishing House, 1964), p. 816.

[10] A. T. Robertson, *Word Pictures in the New Testament* (Grand Rapids: Baker Book House, 1931), 4:456.

CONCLUSION

Summation

We should note some major points of emphasis as this study ends. First, the holiness of God is an awe-inspiring subject. We who know Christ should be overwhelmed by the greatness, majesty, purity, and perfection of the God who created this world, put man here, and revealed Himself to man to redeem him. The thought that the God of holiness dwells with repentant men is humbling. The knowledge that God communicates His holiness to men through Christ when He saves them defies comprehension.

The fact that God's apartness from sin is a part of His holiness is unquestionable. Scripture is equally clear that the separation of the believer from sin is a reflection of God's holiness and is produced by the Spirit of God who uses the Word of God to accomplish it. Furthermore, separation from religious infidelity is an expression by the local church of its desire to reflect God's holiness as it ministers to win lost people to Christ. Finally, separation from brethren is a grievous but necessary action when another believer's lifestyle or compromise with unbelievers reflects upon the purity of the local church. The separatist should reflect God's holiness in his spirit and attitude as well as in his life and ministry.

Applications

Several applications emerge as the truth discussed in this study is assimilated.

Salvation

God is holy, and He transcends man in His holiness. Yet He deigns to dwell with repentant men. He has revealed His holiness in Christ, who died for sinners and is made sanctification to those who trust Him. God communicates His holiness to sinful men in the person of Christ. If one reads this who is not sure of everlasting life, he should trust Christ and receive God's gift of salvation.

Responses to God's Holiness

God's holiness demands certain responses. They have been identified as repentance, joy, worship, gratitude, and a studied imitation of God's holiness. The believer must examine his heart and make sure that he responds properly in action and spirit to God's holiness.

Personal Separation

The Bible's teaching on personal separation means that the believer should actively integrate the holiness of God into his life. He must begin this process by developing a positive desire for holiness. As the Christian studies the Word of God, obeys the Holy Spirit, and learns from God's discipline in his life, he will evidence an increasing purpose to imitate God's holiness and to be like his heavenly Father.

The believer who desires holiness will discipline his thought life accordingly. Purity is to be one of the standards which the Christian imposes upon his thinking. What the believer reads, watches, and listens to should be determined by the purity of its content, along with the other criteria outlined in Philippians 4:8.

The believer should set standards of conduct for his life which are consistent with revealed truth on the subject. Standards of conduct in accordance with God's holiness should not be difficult for the Christian who has responded properly to God's holiness, has a heartfelt desire for holiness, and who disciplines his thought life by standards of holiness.

Believers must realize that evangelism is one of the purposes for living a life of consistent personal separation from sin. Therefore, the believer must earnestly and consistently work for the salvation of lost people in his personal acquaintance. He works and socializes with unsaved people every day. He needs to realize that God has placed him in the world for the purpose of bringing other people to faith in Christ.

Pastors and leaders of other ministries should seek to set standards for their ministries that are consistent with God's holiness.

Ecclesiastical Separation

Pastors and leaders of other ministries must resolve to be consistent with Scripture in separating from false doctrine and false teachers.

Christian leaders must further resolve to give consistent leadership in evangelism as well as separation in their ministries. Compromise with unbelievers unquestionably distorts evangelism, and separation is equally distorted when divorced from evangelism. The pastor who neglects evangelism in his separatist ministry brings deadness to the work. Such a preacher is biblically unbalanced, as is the pastor who unequally yokes with apostates. This study is as much a call to evangelism as to separatism.

Ecumenical evangelism has not gone away. Pastors who seek to obey God must continue to shun it. Christians should resolve not to be part of local church fellowships which cooperate with unbelievers in evangelistic endeavors.

If a believer determines to give to ministries outside his local church, he should be sure that he is supporting ministries that are consistent in their separation and not entangled with false doctrine or false teachers. The Christian might be wiser and safer to give to such projects through his local church with the advice and consent of the pastor and church leadership.

Separation from Christian Brothers

The local church will occasionally have to separate itself from disobedient Christians. In the context of the local church, the individual Christian should follow the leadership of the pastor who biblically seeks the recovery of those who sin and then leads the church to discipline those who will not repent. Pastors, Christian leaders, and laymen must remember that separation from a disobedient brother is always the last resort and that the goal of all actions must be the restoration of those who fall into error.

Local churches and service organizations must also strengthen their purpose to be consistent in the practice of separation from disobedient brethren in matters of fellowship and cooperation. It is always difficult to withhold fellowship from brothers in the Lord.

The standard for practice is not personal friendship but biblical principle. When a brother or a ministry persists in being unequally yoked with unbelievers, espouses false doctrine, or tolerates a lifestyle which is forbidden by Scripture, then the regrettable action of separation must be taken. This must not be done in a hasty or unkind manner. Separatists must remember that the disobedient brother is still a brother.

Biblical Spirit

The Bible's teaching about the spirit of the separatist should prompt serious thought by all who are committed to biblical separatism. Some separatists should be convicted of their lack of a true biblical spirit and resolve to cultivate a proper spirit which is in harmony with what the Bible teaches.

Principled Thinking

This book has approached the subject of separation in a specific way. It has attempted to describe biblical guidelines for the practice of separatism and has also sought to identify the philosophy of New Evangelicalism and to argue against it. It has *not* taken the responsibility of identifying every New Evangelical ministry, leader, or form of compromise. Ministries prosper and then later cease to exist. Leaders come to the forefront and then fade into the background. Different issues demand attention from one year to another. *The purpose of this study has been to deal with the enduring principles which apply in any situation because they are biblical, enduring truths. Pastors and leaders should learn to think for themselves and apply permanent principles to whatever circumstance is current.* Fundamentalists should not think in terms of personalities and organizations but in terms of biblical principle. Local churches should determine their relationship to other churches, to outside organizations, or to leaders by a common loyalty to biblical principle. We desperately need Christian leaders to put the Bible first in their ministries, understand scriptural principles, and minister within the framework of those principles.

Challenges

To Separatists

The preacher who is committed to separatism should take heart that his position is biblical. Scripture not only teaches separation, but it also gives the servant of the Lord a frame of reference for its practice. Preachers should determine again to balance separation and evangelism and seek to glorify God in their ministries. They should purpose to be free of the unequal yoke, and they should kindly refuse to work in cooperation with brothers in the ministry who maintain the unequal yoke or who otherwise disobey clear commands of Scripture. They should also determine before God to manifest a godly spirit in their militant separation. They should again dedicate themselves to the task of teaching biblical holiness to their people and challenging them to imitate God's holiness in their conduct.

To Evangelicals

This study presents a challenge to second- and third-generation preachers who minister and move in the evangelical frame of reference. Harold Ockenga and those with him consciously and purposefully set aside separatism in favor of a strategy of infiltration. That decision was either consistent with Scripture or it was not. This study affirms boldly but without any animosity that it was a decision inconsistent with Scripture.

David Neff, writing from the perspective of the New Evangelicals, speaks of many within the movement who "may be less certain of its direction and identity."[1] Many men within New Evangelicalism love the Lord and His Word. They desire to please Him in their ministries and are persuaded of the inspiration and inerrancy of Scripture. They accept the fact that revealed Scripture is the only measure for an understanding of theology. They should accept the challenge to examine the philosophy of their movement in the light of the Word of God, *and set out on a course of complete obedience to God.*

Notes

[1]David Neff, "A Good First Step," *Christianity Today,* 14 July 1989, p. 15.

Appendix A

ETYMOLOGY AND USES OF BIBLICAL WORDS FOR HOLINESS

Holiness In the Old Testament

The verb קָדַשׁ (*qadash*) and its family of words represent the Hebrew word for holiness.[1] The words are translated as "pure, clean, holy."[2] Universally, lexicographers recognize these translations as accurate. Brown, Driver, and Briggs give the meaning of the words as "holy, sanctuary, cleanse, apartness, sacredness."[3] Koehler and Baumgartner render the words as "be holy, withheld from profane use, holy things, filled with holiness, therefore to be treated carefully."[4]

Etymology of the Word

While there is virtual unanimity among scholars as to the translation and usage of the word, the origin of the word presents some controversy, and that controversy has some bearing on this study.

Louis Berkhof expresses the traditional position as to the root of the words for holiness. He states, "The Hebrew word for 'to be holy,' *quadash,* is derived from the root *qad,* which means to cut or separate."[5] Brown, Driver, and Briggs write of the "possible original idea of separation, withdrawal."[6] Robert Girdlestone says that the word "is used in some form or other to represent being set apart for the work of God."[7] Otto Procksch adopts the same view, stating that the root means "to divide."[8] Ernest Klein, citing seven cognate languages, affirms, "The original meaning of this base probably was 'to separate.' "[9]

The majority of linguists agree on this position. Theologians who have written on the subject of holiness also generally adopt this position. Millard Erickson says: "The Hebrew word for 'holy' . . . means 'marked off' or 'withdrawn from common, ordinary use.' The verb from which it is derived suggests 'to cut off' or 'to separate.' "[10]

In his work on holiness, R. C. Sproul says, "The primary meaning of holy is 'separate.' It comes from an ancient word that meant 'to cut' or 'to separate.' To translate this basic meaning into contemporary language would be to use the phrase 'a cut apart.' Perhaps even more accurate would be the phrase 'a cut above.' "[11]

Although this position is the most widely accepted—and is probably the right conclusion—other views should be presented. Another view which has been long held by scholars is that קָדַשׁ comes from a root which means "shining." This view cannot be summarily rejected, because men whose ability in the Hebrew language is respected hold to this position.

Julius Fuerst advocated the alternative view over a hundred years ago. He believed that the word for holiness comes from a root which means "to be fresh, new, young, of things; to be pure shining, bright, of persons and things. According to this fundamental signification it is commonly equal to 'be holy, consecrated.' "[12]

Koehler and Baumgartner follow this line of reasoning. They cite both Ugaritic and Akkadian roots which are rendered "shine."[13] James Packer apparently adopts this view in its theological import, stating: "Holiness is the outshining of all that God is."[14] Thomas E. McComiskey clearly describes the problem: "The suggestion that the root *qdsh* is derived from an original bilateral *qd* ('cut') is attractive but tenuous in view of the uncertainties surrounding the transmission of bilateral roots to the trilateral form. The meaning 'to separate' is favored . . . but the fact that *qdsh* rarely . . . occurs in a secular sense makes any positive conclusion in this regard difficult."[15]

For the purposes of this study it would be convenient to adopt the former view of the etymology of the words for holiness. To proceed from the root "to cut" or "divide" to the idea of separateness in holiness would be easy and present a strong argument. However, enough evidence exists for the latter view so that the issue is not clear-cut. Objectively, the evidence for the former view is not conclusive beyond reasonable doubt, although the majority of linguists prefer it.

Both ideas will seem to present themselves in the use of the word in the Old Testament. Leviticus 20:26 and verses like it strongly support the idea of "cutting" or "dividing" as the root. On the other hand, verses such as Psalms 96:6-9 and other passages, indicate the idea of "shining" as the root. The preponderance of the evidence leans toward the idea of "cutting," but it appears that the issue cannot be settled beyond question.

One conclusion reached by all scholars in this discussion is that regardless of the etymological source for the words for holiness, the idea of separation is part of the meaning of the word. Indeed, the concept of separation is inherent in the word. Gesenius uses the terms "pure, clean";[16] Brown, Driver, and Briggs speak of "apartness";[17] Koehler and Baumgartner state that the word means "to be holy, withheld from profane use";[18] Klein uses the word "pure,"[19] while Fuerst uses the term "consecrate" to define the word.[20]

Whichever position they adopt, most theological word studies attribute the idea of separation to holiness. J. C. Lambert states: "Etymology gives no sure verdict on the point, but the idea of separation lends itself best to the various senses in which the word 'holiness' is employed."[21] McComiskey states that the word "is distinct from the common or profane."[22] Procksch speaks "of what is marked off from the secular."[23]

Regardless of the root from which the Old Testament word springs, the idea of purity, cleanness, or that which is set apart from the profane and unto God is carried within it. The idea of separation is an essential part of the concept of holiness.

Uses of the Word

The קָדַשׁ (*qdsh*) family of words represents the idea of holiness, and, as stated above, separation is a vital ingredient in the concept. A survey of the uses of the word throughout the Old Testament shows that the words are used in several relationships.

Of God

The holiness of God is affirmed in several ways. God in revealing Himself to men states that He is holy (Lev. 11:44; 19:2). Scripture declares that His name is holy (Lev. 22:2; Ps. 111:9; Isa. 57:15). The Spirit of God is occasionally called holy (Ps. 51:11; Isa. 63:10-11). God's holiness distinguishes Him from man (I Sam. 2:2). His works are holy (Ps. 145:17), and His word is declared to be holy (Pss. 89:35; 105:42; Jer. 23:9; Amos 4:2).[24]

Of Angels

The angels are referred to by the term "saints" or קְדֹשִׁים (qedoshim)—"holy ones" (Job 15:15; Ps. 89:6-8; Dan. 8:13).[25]

Of Places

Heaven, the dwelling place of God, is called holy (II Chron. 30:27; Ps. 68:5; Isa. 57:15). Places where God appeared to men are called holy (Exod. 3:5; Josh. 5:15). The tabernacle (Exod. 40:9), the temple (II Chron. 7:16; 29:7), and Jerusalem (Ps. 48:1-2) are identified as holy.

Of Things

Numbers of inanimate objects are identified as holy in the Old Testament. Among these are the altar (Exod. 29:37; 30:10), and the vessels of the tabernacle (Josh. 6:19).

Of Time

God declared the Sabbath day to be holy (Gen. 2:3) and commanded that it be kept holy (Exod. 20:8-11).

Of People

Israel as God's chosen nation is called holy (Exod. 19:6; Isa. 63:18). The priests set apart for God's service are called holy (Exod. 30:29; Lev. 21:6-8). Elisha was perceived as "an holy man of God" (II Kings 4:9), and the Nazirites who separated themselves to God were called holy (Num. 6:5-8). Individuals who fear God are called holy as well (Pss. 16:3; 34:9). God calls His people to a lifestyle which imitates His holiness (Lev. 19:2). He then prescribes positive action and proscribes sinful action (Lev. 19:3–20:25). He is holy, and His people are to refrain from evil because they are His (Lev. 20:26).

Holiness in the New Testament

The Greek verb ἁγιάζω (*hagiazō*) and its related words are "the Greek representative of *Kadash*."[26] A related word, ἁγνός (*hagnos*), shares the same root.[27]

Etymology of the Word

While the etymology of the word is not certain,[28] it is linked to ἅγος (*hagos*), which was used in secular writing for veneration, or reverence, of the gods or parents.[29] In the New Testament, the words are translated "make holy," "consecrate," "sanctify," "purify," "holy," or "holiness."[30] Trench says, "Its fundamental idea is separation, and so to speak, consecration and devotion to the service of Deity."[31] The New Testament concept of holiness presumes the preceding revelation of the Old Testament.[32]

Uses of the Word

The idea of holiness is used in reference to the Godhead, to people, and to things in the New Testament.

Of Things

As in the Old Testament, Jerusalem is called the holy city (Matt. 4:5). Jesus referred to the "holy place" in the temple (Matt. 24:15). The Mount of Transfiguration is called the "holy mount" (II Pet. 1:18). The dwelling of God in heaven is called the "holy place" (Heb. 9:12). Other places or things are called holy, but these references are less numerous in the New Testament than in the Old. The reason is that the old economy emphasized the ceremonial, while the new emphasizes the spiritual. Places are called holy because God manifested His presence there (e.g., II Pet. 1:18).

Of Angels

On a few occasions angels—who will accompany Christ at His return (Mark 8:38), who brought God's revelation to men (Acts 10:22), and who will observe judgment (Rev. 14:10)—are called holy.

Of God

Although holiness is not attributed to God as frequently in the New Testament as in the Old, the truth of God's holiness is taught. Building upon the passage in Leviticus 17-26, which Stanley Chestnut calls "The Holiness Code,"[33] Peter quotes Leviticus 19:2 and affirms that God is holy (I Pet. 1:15). Jesus called God the "Holy Father" (John 17:11). In a scene reminiscent of Isaiah 6, the living creatures with six wings worship the thrice-holy God (Rev. 4:8).

Of Christ

Christ is called holy (Acts 3:14; 4:27, 30), His character is declared to be holy (Rev. 3:7), and His equality with God in holiness is acknowledged by an unclean spirit (Mark 1:23-24). Peter declares His holiness (John 6:69). It should be noted that the Greek construction in this passage is exactly the same as in Revelation 6:10, where it refers to the Father. These passages teach the deity of Christ and His equality with God[34] in holiness and truthfulness.

Of the Spirit of God

Holiness is infrequently used of the Spirit in the Old Testament. The basis for the Spirit's being called "the Holy Spirit" in the Old Testament is Psalm 51:11 and Isaiah 63:10.[35] In the New Testament the Spirit is often identified by this title (Matt. 1:18, 20; 3:11). In fact, this term is used of the Spirit of God ninety-three times in the New Testament.[36]

Of Scripture

Scripture and the men who were inspired of the Holy Spirit to write it are identified as holy (Rom. 1:2; II Pet. 1:21).

Of People

In the New Testament select groups of people are called holy because of their service for God. The prophets (Luke 1:70; II Pet. 3:2); John the Baptist (Mark 6:20); and certain Old Testament women, especially Sarah, are known as holy (I Pet. 3:5-6). The apostles and prophets of the New Testament era are also spoken of as holy (Eph. 3:5). The New Testament also refers to believers as holy. This last usage is so comprehensive, however, that it merits a separate discussion in the following section.

Of Believers

The New Testament predicates holiness in the life of the believer upon his relationship to Christ. The believer is sanctified by the finished work of Christ (Heb. 10:10) and receives that holiness by faith in Christ (Acts 26:18). The believer is sanctified (set apart) and called a saint (holy) because of his relationship to Christ (I Cor. 1:2). Not only does the believer receive righteousness and redemption in Christ, but he also receives sanctification (I Cor. 1:30). Holiness is a part of God's work of salvation in the believer.

Because holiness is part of salvation, the believer is holy in his standing before God. Believers are called holy (I Cor. 3:17; I Thess. 5:27; Heb. 3:1; I Pet. 2:9) and are repeatedly called saints (Rom. 1:7; I Cor. 1:2; Eph. 1:1; Phil. 1:1; 4:21).

The ultimate purpose of God for the believer in eternity is holiness (I Thess. 3:13; Col. 1:22). In the present life, holiness in practice is the purpose of God for the believer (Rom. 12:1-2; Eph. 1:4; I Pet. 1:15; II Pet. 3:11). Since the believer is called to holiness (I Thess. 4:7; II Tim. 1:9), holiness is to be the pursuit of his life (Heb. 12:14).

Once he is saved, the believer participates in the process of sanctification. At salvation he receives the holiness of God and is positionally holy, but as he consciously "depart[s] from iniquity" (II Tim. 2:19) and cleanses himself, he is "sanctified" for God's use (II Tim. 2:21).

The means which God uses to produce holiness in the life of the believer are many. Holiness of life is always the product of the righteousness of God which is received by faith in Christ (Mark 6:20; I Cor. 1:30; Rom. 6:19, 22). The Word of God produces holiness (John 17:17; Eph. 5:26). The fear of God produces the perfection of this holiness in the believer's life (II Cor. 7:1). God's discipline of the believer produces holiness so the believer might "share in His holy character."[37]

The holy standing received when one is justified by faith will result in a lifestyle of holiness (Rev. 22:11).

Purity and Holiness

The concept of purity is closely related to holiness. The word ἁγνός (*hagnos*) is, in fact, from the same root as the word for holiness. Girdlestone states that the Greek word "answers very well to our word purity, in its double sense of chastity and freedom from wrong motives."[38] This concept is used in several ways in Scripture.

Of Christ

In I John 3:3 the believer is called to purify himself in the imitation of Christ who is pure.

Of Believers

The Bible urges purity upon believers in their lives and relationships with others (II Cor. 6:6; I Tim. 4:12; 5:2; I Pet. 3:2).

Repentance from sin produces this purity (II Cor. 7:11). Purity should be characteristic of the believer's thought life (Phil. 4:8). Paul viewed the Corinthian church as a pure virgin, to be presented to Christ (II Cor. 11:2).

Of God's Wisdom

James declares, "But the wisdom that is from above is first pure" (James 3:17). When one compares James 1:5 and 3:17, James appears to speak of the wisdom which God promises to those who ask.

Consecration and Holiness

The idea of holiness is occasionally conveyed through the word ἱερός (*hieros*) and its derivatives. Consecration is the fundamental idea of this word.[39] The words in the group are used in the New Testament to refer to a person's demeanor (Titus 2:3), which is to be befitting holiness; to Scripture (II Tim. 3:15); to the holy work of the temple (I Cor. 9:13); and to the ministry of the gospel (Rom. 15:16). The word and its derivatives throughout the New Testament also refer to temples, whether God's temple in Jerusalem or heathen temples. The idea of separation is inherent in the word. It denotes that which is set apart by God for His service or by the heathen for the use of an idol.

Piety and Holiness

Another word, ὅσιος (*hosios*), is also used for holiness. It conveys the idea of holiness as devoutness or piety.[40] Thayer defines it further as meaning "undefiled by sin, free from wickedness, observing every moral obligation, pure, holy, pious."[41] The word is used of God, quoting Old Testament passages in Revelation 15:3-4 (Ps. 145:17) and Revelation 16:5 (Deut. 32:4). The word is also used of Christ (Heb. 7:26; Acts 2:27; 13:35). In Acts 13:34 it is used in a quotation of Isaiah 55:3, "the sure mercies of David."[42]

This word is also used twice in reference to a person's lifestyle. On both occasions it is used in conjunction with righteousness (Luke 1:75; Eph. 4:24). By definition and usage, separation is a part of the concept. The word speaks of a piety which is in Christ and is produced in the believer's life by the righteousness of God. It stands in dramatic contrast to sin.

Notes

[1]Samuel P. Tregelles, *Gesenius' Hebrew and Chaldee Lexicon To the Old Testament Scriptures* (Grand Rapids: Eerdmans, n.d.), p. 725.

[2]Ibid.

[3]Francis Brown, S. R. Driver, and Charles A. Briggs, *A Hebrew and English Lexicon of the Old Testament* (Oxford: Clarendon Press, 1979), p. 871.

[4]Ludwig Koehler and Walter Baumgartner, *Lexicon In Veteris Testamenti Libros* (Grand Rapids: Eerdmans, 1951), pp. 825-27.

[5]Louis Berkhof, *Systematic Theology* (Grand Rapids: Eerdmans, 1941), p. 73.

[6]Brown, Driver, Briggs, p. 871.

[7]Robert Baker Girdlestone, *Synonyms of the Old Testament* (Grand Rapids: Eerdmans, 1976 reprint), p. 175.

[8]Otto Procksch, "ἅγιος," *Theological Dictionary of the New Testament,* ed. Gerhard Kittel (Grand Rapids: Eerdmans, 1974), 1:89.

[9]Ernest Klein, *A Comprehensive Etymological Dictionary of the Hebrew Language for Readers of English* (New York: MacMillan Publishing Co., 1987), p. 284.

[10]Millard J. Erickson, *Christian Theology* (Grand Rapids: Baker Book House, 1985), p. 284.

[11]R.C. Sproul, *The Holiness of God* (Wheaton: Tyndale House Publishers, 1988), p. 54.

[12]Julius Fuerst, *A Hebrew and Chaldee Lexicon to the Old Testament* (London: Williams and Norgate, 1871), p. 1221.

[13]Koehler and Baumgartner, p. 825.

[14]James Packer, "God Is," *Eerdmans' Handbook To Christian Belief,* ed. Robin Keeley (Grand Rapids: Eerdmans, 1982), p. 136.

[15]Thomas E. McComiskey, "קָדֹש‎," *Theological Wordbook of the Old Testament,* ed. R. Laird Harris (Chicago: Moody Press), 1980, 2:786-87.

[16]Tregelles, p. 725.

[17]Brown, Driver, Briggs, p. 871.

[18]Koehler, Baumgartner, p. 825.

[19]Klein, p. 563.

[20]Fuerst, p. 1221.

[21]J. C. Lambert, "Holiness," *International Standard Bible Encyclopaedia,* ed. James Orr (Grand Rapids: Eerdmans, 1960 reprint), 3:1403.

[22]McComiskey, 2:786.

[23]Procksch, 1:89.

[24]It should be noted that God's Word in each of the above cases refers to a specific revelation to an individual, not to the entire body of Scripture. The truth revealed to David, Abraham, Jeremiah, or Amos was later inscripturated, but the holy word in each case refers to the specific revelation to each man. These verses should not necessarily be taken as proof texts for the holiness of the entire body of revealed, inspired truth. That body of truth is also declared to be holy (Rom. 1:2; II Tim. 3:15).

[25]The adjective is also used of men who fear the Lord (Ps. 16:3). The context of the verses cited indicates that angelic beings are referred to and identified as "holy ones."

[26]W. E. Vine, *Vine's Expository Dictionary of New Testament Words* (McLean: MacDonald Publishing Company, n.d.), pp. 565-67.

[27]Girdlestone, p. 179.

[28]Richard Chenevix Trench, *Synonyms of the New Testament* (Grand Rapids: Eerdmans, 1963), p. 331.

[29]Colin Brown, "ἅγιος," *The New International Dictionary of New Testament Theology,* ed. Colin Brown (Grand Rapids: Zondervan, 1970), 2:224.

[30]Joseph Henry Thayer, *Greek English Lexicon of the New Testament* (Grand Rapids: Zondervan, 1970), p. 6.

[31]Trench, p. 331.

[32]Procksch, 1:100.

[33]J. Stanley Chestnut, *The Old Testament Understanding of God* (Philadelphia: Westminster Press, 1968), p. 133.

[34]Procksch, 1:102.

[35]Ibid., 1:103.

[36]Robert Young, *Analytical Concordance to the Bible* (Grand Rapids: Eerdmans, n.d.), p. 488.

[37]William F. Arndt and F. Wilbur Gingrich, *A Greek-English Lexicon of the New Testament* (Chicago: University of Chicago Press, 1957), p. 10.

[38]Girdlestone, p. 181.

[39]Thayer, p. 229, defines the word as "sacred, consecrated to the deity, pertaining to God." H. Seebass, "ἱερός," *New International Dictionary of New Testament Theology,* 2:232, defines it in part as "consecrated by divine power."

[40]Seebass, p. 236.

[41]Thayer, p. 456.

[42]Seebass, p. 238.

Appendix B

HAROLD JOHN OCKENGA'S PRESS RELEASE ON "THE NEW EVANGELICALISM"

FOR RELEASE

6:00 P.M.; Sunday

December 8, 1957

"The New Evangelicalism"

Rev. Dr. Harold John Ockenga

"The churches which represent orthodox religion today dare to handle social problems which the Fundamentalists avoided: racial integration, crime, mental health, moral disintegration, and narcotics," an international church leader said tonight.

"Fundamentalism," he charged, "abdicated leadership and responsibility in the societal realm."

"The New Evangelicalism is the application of historic Christian faith to the social problems of our day," declared the Rev. Dr. Harold John Ockenga, chairman of the International Commission of the National Association of Evangelicals (headquarters in Washington, D.C.) representing 65,000 churches throughout the world with a membership of some 20 million Protestants.

Dr. Ockenga who is the originator of the new movement explained that the New Evangelicalism "differs from Fundamentalism in its willingness to handle the social problems which the Fundamentalists evaded.

"There need be no disagreement between the personal gospel and the social gospel. The true Christian faith is a supernatural personal experience of salvation and a social philosophy. Doctrine and social ethics are Christian disciplines."

Dr. Ockenga pointed out in the concluding address of his Sunday evening series of discussions on important social problems which marked his 21st anniversary as pastor of historic Park Street Church in Boston, that the strategy of the New Evangelicalism has changed from one of separation to infiltration.

"The strategy of evangelicalism is the positive proclamation of the truth in distinction from all errors without delving in personalities which embrace the error. The evangelical believes that Christianity is intellectually defensible, but the Christian cannot be obscurantist in scientific questions pertaining to the creation, the age of man, the universality of the flood and other debatable Biblical questions. The evangelical attempts to apply Christian truth to every phrase of life.

"The New Evangelicalism is willing to face the intellectual problems and meet them in the framework of modern learning. It stands doctrinally upon the creeds and confession of the Church and grants liberty in minor areas when discussion is promoted on the basis of exegesis of Scripture."

Dr. Ockenga referred to the four or five decades in which Fundamentalism has embraced the literal view of the Bible as being God's revelation and trustworthy, that Jesus Christ is the Son of God, that the miracles performed by Christ were evidences of the supernatural, that the death of Jesus Christ on the cross was an atonement for sin, that the resurrection of Christ was a literal bodily resurrection, and that salvation is by faith.

"The Modernists," he asserted, "advanced a different meaning for the Bible, for Christ, and for every historic Christian truth. Basing its theology upon the teaching of higher criticism, Modernism accommodated its teachings to the modern mind and explained away the supernatural, the mysteries of the Christian faith and the necessity of regeneration. The only permanent values resided in faith, love, hope and similar graces," the clergyman said.

"Evangelicalism must be identified with the orthodox branch of the historical Church," the noted theologian continued, "and the

New Evangelicalism is the infusion of the social emphasis into this theology."

Dr. Ockenga, who is President of the Board of Trustees of Fuller Theological Seminary (Pasadena, Cal.), said that since he first coined the phrase "The New Evangelicalism" ten years ago at a convocation address at the seminary, the evangelical forces have been welded into a world-wide organizational front of some 20 million members in 26 countries.

"First," he said, "there is the National Association of Evangelicals which provides articulation for the movement on the denominational level.

"Second, there is the World Evangelical Fellowship which binds together these individual national associations," explained the concurrent Chairman of both organizations.

"Third, there is the new apologetic literature stating this point of view which is now flowing from the presses of leading publishers (Macmillans and Harpers).

"Fourth, there is the existence of Fuller Theological Seminary and other evangelical seminaries fully committed to orthodox Christianity and a resultant social philosophy.

"Fifth, to further articulate the convictions of this movement," Dr. Ockenga who is President of the Board of Directors referred to the establishment of *Christianity Today,* a bi-weekly publication (Washington, D.C.—world's largest circulation to ministers—over 160,000).

"Sixth, there is the appearance of an evangelist, Billy Graham, who on the mass level is the spokesman of the convictions and deals of the New Evangelicalism."

SELECTED BIBLIOGRAPHY

Books and Commentaries

Alford, Henry. *The Greek New Testament*. Cambridge: Deighton, Bell, and Co., 1877.

Armerding, Carl E. "Habakkuk." In *The Expositor's Bible Commentary*, vol. 7. Edited by Frank E. Gaebelein. Grand Rapids: Zondervan, 1985.

Ashbrook, John E. *Axioms of Separation*. Mentor, Ohio: "Here I Stand" Books, n.d.

Ashbrook, William E. *Evangelicalism, The New Neutralism*. Mentor, Ohio: John E. Ashbrook, 9th printing, n.d.

Barnes, Albert. *Thessalonians—Philemon*. Notes on the New Testament. Reprint. Grand Rapids: Baker Book House, 1979.

Berkhof, Louis. *Systematic Theology*. Grand Rapids: Eerdmans, 1941.

Bob Jones University, Bible Faculty. *Biblical Separation*. Greenville, S.C.: Bob Jones University Press, 1980.

Bruce, Alexander Balmain. "Matthew." In *The Expositor's Greek New Testament*, vol. 1. Edited by W. Robertson Nicoll. Reprint. Grand Rapids: Eerdmans, 1976.

Bruce, F. F. *The Epistle to the Ephesians*. Reprint. Old Tappan, N.J.: Fleming H. Revell Company, 1974.

Chafer, Lewis Sperry. *Systematic Theology*. Dallas: Dallas Seminary Press, 1948.

Chestnut, J. Stanley. *The Old Testament Understanding of God*. Philadelphia: Westminster Press, 1968.

DeHaan, Kurt. *I'm Not A Legalist, Am I?* Grand Rapids: Radio Bible Class, 1988.

Eadie, John. *Commentary on the Epistle to the Ephesians.* Reprint. Grand Rapids: Zondervan, 1979.

Erdman, Charles R. *The General Epistles.* Philadelphia: Westminster Press, 1919.

Erickson, Millard J. *Christian Theology.* Grand Rapids: Baker Book House, 1985.

Fairbairn, Patrick. *Pastoral Epistles.* Reprint. Minneapolis: Klock and Klock Christian Publishers, Inc., 1980.

Findley, G. G. "St. Paul's First Epistle to the Corinthians." In *The Expositor's Greek New Testament,* vol. 2. Edited by W. Robertson Nicoll. Reprint. Grand Rapids: Eerdmans, 1983.

Ginsburg, C. D. "Leviticus." In *Ellicott's Commentary on the Whole Bible,* vol. 1. Edited by Charles John Ellicott. Grand Rapids: Zondervan, 1954 edition.

Guthrie, Donald. *The Pastoral Epistles.* Grand Rapids: Eerdmans, 1964.

Hendricksen, William. *Exposition of Ephesians.* New Testament Commentary. Reprint. Grand Rapids: Baker Book House, 1979.

————. *Exposition of Pastoral Epistles.* New Testament Commentary. Reprint. Grand Rapids: Baker Book House, 1978.

Hiebert, D. Edmond. *First Timothy.* Chicago: Moody Press, 1957.

————. *Second Timothy.* Chicago: Moody Press, 1957.

————. *The Thessalonian Epistles.* Reprint. Chicago: Moody Press, 1982.

Hodge, Charles. *An Exposition of the First Epistle to the Corinthians.* Reprint. Grand Rapids: Eerdmans, 1974.

————. *Commentary on the Second Epistle to the Corinthians.* Grand Rapids: Eerdmans, n.d.

————. *Systematic Theology.* Reprint. Grand Rapids: Eerdmans, 1977.

Hughes, Philip Edgecumbe. *Paul's Epistles to the Corinthians.* The New International Commentary on the New Testament, edited by Ned B. Stonehouse. Grand Rapids: Eerdmans, 1962.

Hutson, Curtis. *New Evangelicalism, An Enemy of Fundamentalism.* Murfreesboro: Sword of the Lord Publishers, 1984.

————. *Unnecessary Divisions Among Fundamentalists.* Murfreesboro: Sword of the Lord Publishers, 1990.

Jackson, Paul R. *The Position, Attitudes and Objectives of Biblical Separation*. Des Plaines, Ill.: General Association of Regular Baptist Churches, n.d.

Kelly, J.N.D. *A Commentary on the Epistles of Peter and Jude*. Reprint. Grand Rapids: Baker Book House, 1981.

Kent, Homer A., Jr. *The Pastoral Epistles*. Chicago: Moody Press, 1958.

———. "Philippians." In *The Expositor's Bible Commentary,* vol. 9. Edited by Frank E. Gaebelein. Grand Rapids: Zondervan, 1985.

Knapp, George Christian. *Lectures on Christian Theology*. Philadelphia: J. W. Moore, 1851.

Lenski, R.C.H. *The Interpretation of St. Matthew's Gospel*. Minneapolis: Augsburg Publishing House, 1964.

———. *The Interpretation of I and II Corinthians*. Minneapolis: Augsburg Publishing House, 1963.

———. *The Interpretation of St. Paul's Epistles to the Colossians, to the Thessalonians, to Timothy, to Titus, and to Philemon*. Minneapolis: Augsburg Publishing House, 1964.

McCune, Rolland. *Ecclesiastical Separation*. Detroit: Detroit Baptist Theological Seminary, n.d.

Miley, John. *Systematic Theology*. New York: Eaton and Mains, 1892.

Moule, H.C.G. *Ephesian Studies*. London: Pickering and Inglis, n.d.

Müller, Jac. J. *The Epistles of Paul to the Philippians and Philemon*. Grand Rapids: Eerdmans, 1955.

Ockenga, Harold John. Introduction to *The Battle for the Bible*, by Harold Lindsell. Grand Rapids: Zondervan, 1976.

———. *The Epistles to the Thessalonians*. Proclaiming the New Testament. Grand Rapids: Baker Book House, 1962.

Pickering, Ernest. *Biblical Separation: The Struggle for a Pure Church*. Schaumburg: Regular Baptist Press, 1979.

———. *Should We Ever Separate from Christian Brethren?* Minneapolis: Central Press, n.d.

Plumtre, E. H., and Whitelaw, T. *Ezekiel*. The Pulpit Commentary. Edited by H.D.M. Spence and Joseph S. Exell. Grand Rapids: Eerdmans, 1962.

Pope, William Burt. *A Compendium of Christian Theology*. New York: Phillips and Hunt, n.d.

Robertson, A. T. *Word Pictures in the New Testament,* vol. 4. Grand Rapids: Baker Book House, 1931.

Ryrie, Charles C. *Basic Theology.* Wheaton: Victor Books, 1986.

Shedd, William G. T. *Dogmatic Theology.* Grand Rapids: Zondervan, n.d.

Sproul, R. C. *The Holiness of God.* Wheaton: Tyndale House Publishers, Inc., 1988.

Strong, Augustus Hopkins. *Systematic Theology.* Valley Forge: Judson Press, 1907.

Swindoll, Charles R. *The Grace Awakening.* Dallas: Word Publishing, 1990.

Thiessen, Henry C. *Lectures in Systematic Theology.* Grand Rapids: Eerdmans, 1949.

Thompson, James. *The Second Letter to the Corinthians.* The Living Word Commentary, edited by Everett Ferguson. Austin: R. B. Sweet Co., Inc., 1970.

Van Gorder, Paul R. *The Church Stands Corrected.* Wheaton: Victor Books, 1976.

Van Impe, Jack. *Heart Disease in Christ's Body.* Royal Oak, Mich.: Jack Van Impe Ministries, 1984.

Vincent, M. R. *Word Studies in the New Testament,* vol. 2. McDill AFB, Fla.: MacDonald Publishing Company, n.d.

Vine, W. E. *Exposition of the Epistles to Timothy.* London: Pickering and Inglis, 1925.

Watson, Thomas. *A Body of Divinity.* Reprint. London: Banner of Truth Trust, 1970.

Wiersbe, Warren W. *The Bible Exposition Commentary.* 2 vols. Wheaton: Victor Books, 1989.

Wood, A. Skevington. "Ephesians." In *The Expositor's Bible Commentary,* vol. 11. Edited by Frank E. Gaebelein. Grand Rapids: Zondervan, 1985.

Wuest, Kenneth S. "First Peter." In *Wuest's Word Studies from the Greek New Testament,* vol. 2. Reprint. Grand Rapids: Eerdmans, 1980.

Reference Works

Arndt, William F., and Gingrich, F. Wilbur. *A Greek-English Lexicon of the New Testament.* Chicago: University of Chicago Press, 1957.

Brown, Colin, ed. "ἅγιος." In *The New International Dictionary of New Testament Theology*. Grand Rapids: Zondervan, 1970.

Brown, Francis; Driver, S. R.; and Briggs, Charles A. *A Hebrew and English Lexicon of the Old Testament*. Oxford: Clarendon Press, 1979.

Fuerst, Julius. *A Hebrew and Chaldee Lexicon to the Old Testament*. London: Williams and Norgate, 1871.

Girdlestone, Robert Baker. *Synonyms of the Old Testament*. Reprint. Grand Rapids: Eerdmans, 1976.

Goldberg, Louis "חלל." In *Theological Word Book of the Old Testament*. Edited by R. Laird Harris. Chicago: Moody Press, 1980.

Grundmann, Walter. "κακός." In *Theological Dictionary of the New Testament*. Edited by Gerhard Kittel. Grand Rapids: Eerdmans, 1974.

Kellerman, Dana F., ed. *New Webster's Dictionary of the English Language*. New York: Delair Publishing Company, Inc., 1981.

Klein, Ernest. *A Comprehensive Etymological Dictionary of the Hebrew Language for Readers of English*. New York: MacMillan Publishing Co., 1987.

Koehler, Ludwig, and Baumgartner, Walter. *Lexicon In Veteris Testamenti Libros*. Grand Rapids: Eerdmans, 1951.

Lambert, J. C. "Holiness." *International Standard Bible Encyclopaedia*. Edited by James Orr. Grand Rapids: Eerdmans, 1960.

McComiskey, Thomas E. "קדש." In *Theological Word Book of the Old Testament*. Edited by R. Laird Harris. Chicago: Moody Press, 1980.

Packer, James. "God Is." In *Eerdman's Handbook to Christian Belief*. Edited by Robin Keeley. Grand Rapids: Eerdmans, 1982.

Procksch, Otto. "ἅγιος." In *Theological Dictionary of the New Testament*. Edited by Gerhard Kittel. Grand Rapids: Eerdmans, 1974.

Seebass, H. "ἱερός." *The New International Dictionary of New Testament Theology*. Edited by Colin Brown. Grand Rapids: Zondervan, 1970.

Thayer, Joseph Henry. *Greek English Lexicon of the New Testament*. Grand Rapids: Zondervan, 1970.

Tregelles, Samuel P. *Gesenius' Hebrew and Chaldee Lexicon to the Old Testament Scriptures*. Grand Rapids: Eerdmans, n.d.

Trench, Richard Chenevix. *Synonyms of the New Testament*. Reprint. Grand Rapids: Zondervan, 1963.

Unger, Merrill F. *The New Unger's Bible Dictionary*. Revised edition. Edited by R. K. Harrison. Chicago: Moody Press, 1988.

Vine, W. E. *Vine's Expository Dictionary of New Testament Words.* McLean: MacDonald Publishing Company, n.d.

Young, Robert. *Analytical Concordance to the Bible.* Grand Rapids: Eerdmans, n.d.

Journals and Magazines

Barnhouse, Donald Grey. "One Church." *Eternity,* July 1958, p. 20.

————. "Thanksgiving and Warning." *Eternity,* September 1957, p. 9.

Compton, R. Bruce. "2 Thessalonians 3:6-15 and Biblical Separation." *The Sentinel,* Fall 1988, p. 2.

Delnay, Robert. "Ecclesiastical Separation." *The Faith Pulpit,* June-August 1987, p. 2.

Groothuis, Douglas. "Confronting the New Age." *Christianity Today,* 13 January 1989, p. 36.

Handford, Walter E. "Is Dr. Barnhouse Right?" *Sword of the Lord,* 24 January 1958, p. 1.

Hutson, Curtis. "Questions Answered by the Editor." *Sword of the Lord,* 11 November 1988, n.p.

"Is Evangelical Theology Changing?" *Christian Life,* March 1956, p. 2.

Lightner, Robert P. "A Biblical Perspective on False Doctrine." *Bibliotheca Sacra,* 142 (January-March 1985): 16-22.

McLachlan, Douglas R. "Charting a Straight Course (II)—Legalism." *The Central Testimony,* Winter 1987, p. 1.

Moritz, Frederick James. "Church as Body." *Calvary Baptist Theological Journal* 6 (Spring 1988): 1-24.

Neff, David. "A Good First Step." *Christianity Today,* 14 July 1989, p. 15.

Pulliam, Ken R. "Christian Standards Are Not Legalism." *Front-line,* September-October 1991, p. 7.

Sumner, R. L. "Review of *A Basic Library for Bible Students* by Warren Wiersbe." *Sword of the Lord,* 20 November 1981, p. 6.

Talley, John D. "The Basis for Ecclesiastical Separation." *The Fundamentalist Journal,* April 1983, p. 52.

Unpublished Works

Dissertations

Bixby, Don W. "Separation: In Search of Balance." Class paper, Central Baptist Theological Seminary, 1990.

Holland, John Steward. "A Biblical Theology of Separation." Ph.D. dissertation, Bob Jones University, 1976.

Jaeggli, John Randolph. "An Historical-Theological Analysis of the Holy One of Israel in Isaiah Forty Through Sixty-Six." Ph.D. dissertation, Bob Jones University, 1987.

Zempel, Thomas L. "A Biblical Approach to Understanding the Physical Handicap of Down's Syndrome." D.Min. project, Westminster Theological Seminary, 1990.

Interviews

Ollila, Les, President of Northland Baptist Bible College. Interview by author, 22 November 1991, Dunbar, Wis.

Parker, John Monroe, General Director of Baptist World Mission. Interview by author, 18 December 1991, Decatur, Ala.

Bibles

King James Version. *The Holy Bible Containing the Old and New Testaments.* Nashville: Holman Bible Publishers, 1979.

Nestle, Eberhard, ed. *Novum Testamentum Graece.* Stuttgart: Biblia P.W.B., 1960.

New King James Bible. Nashville: Thomas Nelson Publishers, 1980.

Online Bible Version 5.0. Woodside Bible Fellowship, Elmira, Ont.

Scofield, C. I., ed. *The Scofield Reference Bible.* New York: Oxford University Press, 1909, 1917.

Miscellaneous

Know Your Roots: Evangelicalism Yesterday, Today, and Tomorrow. 2 Hours. 2100 Productions, 1991. Videocassette.

Lee, Tim, to R. L. Hymers, letter, 24 May 1990. Photocopied.

Ockenga, Harold John. Press release. Boston: The Park Street Church, 8 December 1957.

TOPICAL INDEX

SCRIPTURE INDEX